Haunted
Places
of
Cheshire

On the Trail of the Paranormal

Jeffrey Pearson

D1465261

COUNTRYSIDE BOOKS
NEWBURY BERKSHIRE

First published 2006
© Jeffrey Pearson 2006

COUNTRYSIDE BOOKS
3 Catherine Road
Newbury, Berks

To view our complete range of books,
please visit us at
www.countrysidebooks.co.uk

ISBN 1 85306 997 3
EAN 978 1 85306 997 0

For our grandchildren, Lydia, Callum and Oliver

Designed by Peter Davies, Nautilus Design
Produced through MRM Associates Ltd., Reading
Printed by Borcombe Printers plc, Romsey

·Contents·

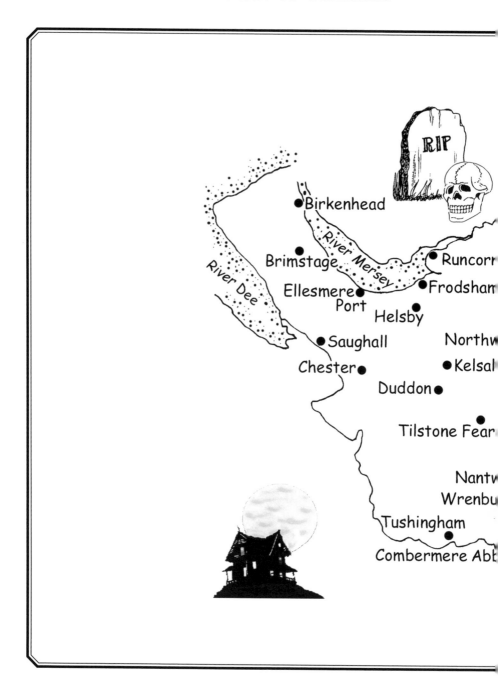

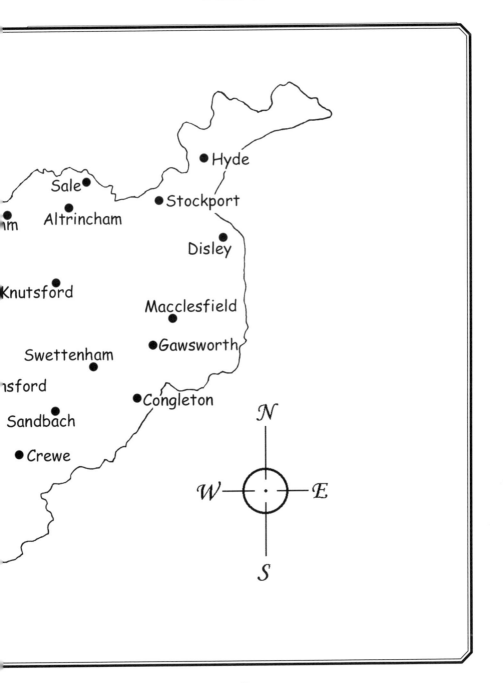

•Introduction•

To the best of my knowledge, I've never seen a ghost or personally encountered any other evidence of the supernatural. Even so, after many years of scepticism, I came to believe that ghosts – apparitions and other active spirits – do exist.

It was our younger daughter, Vicky, who presented my wife, Margaret, and me with the most convincing fragment of evidence that we are ever likely to collect – short of knowingly meeting a spectre head-on. One day, when Vicky was about 12 months old, and just managing a very few words, she was sitting on her mother's knee in the dining room. Suddenly, she pointed. 'Lady!' she exclaimed, and proceeded to follow, with her pointing finger, the progress of some figure, invisible to Margaret, across the room. Obviously, the child knew nothing of ghosts and was simply stating what she could see. Margaret found the incident very disturbing but, at the time, we were obliged to dismiss it as just one of those things which we would never be able to explain.

Now, following a number of similar incidents scattered over the 36 years that have passed since that day, including a recent occasion when Vicky again found herself face-to-face with a ghost, we believe that, as a baby, she saw an apparition.

In the course of my research for this book I've travelled the length and breadth of the historic county of Cheshire, from Birkenhead in the west to Disley in the east and from Sale in the north to Combermere in the south, and I have spoken to many folk who've experienced the paranormal first-hand.

I've learned something of the nature of ghosts and their relationship with the living. For example, I discovered that my wife's experience with baby Vicky was typical of an apparition sighting in two respects. Firstly, that one person could see the ghost while another person present could not and, secondly, that a ghost can appear to be a solid, flesh and blood, individual, and not necessarily the misty figure so beloved by film-makers and book-illustrators. At least, it seems reasonable to believe so, because, in this instance, there was nothing in the way the child spoke to indicate that she could see anything unusual about the ghostly woman. Indeed, from all accounts, it would seem that most apparitions do appear to be living people, and there are even reports of ghosts who have held conversations with unsuspecting folk. There is, however, evidence enough that some apparitions do appear as semi-transparent figures (witness the photograph of Lord Combermere's alleged ghost on page 23).

If the Combermere picture is genuine, capturing it was a remarkable stroke of luck. It is commonly accepted among psychics that it is extremely rare for an apparition to register on a film or memory card – even when the photographer has had the opportunity of focussing directly on it. Possibly that is why ghosts are only very occasionally recorded by CCTV cameras. Or, again possibly, such cameras have captured ghosts but, because the vast majority of apparitions appear to be living people, the images have not been recognised for what they really are.

Paranormal investigators have listed several well-established ways in which spirits can materialise, other than by appearing in human form. The most common is as semi-transparent balls of light, known as 'orbs.' They are next to impossible to see with the naked eye, but are often caught on camera or video recorder, hovering or travelling erratically through the air in old buildings (see the photograph of orbs caught on camera at the Greyhound, Saughall, on page 72). Another way in which spirits can materialise is as a grey, white, or black formless mist. Such mists usually appear a few feet above the ground and can linger or travel quickly (see the photograph of a mist on the stairs at the Railway Inn, Nantwich, on page 55). Another, more specific, type of spirit-mist takes the form of a vortex, which usually appears as a swirling funnel, and typically moves about restlessly, passing through obstacles such as doors and walls. Finally, among these alternative forms of visual ghosts, there

Members of the Supernatural Encounters Association (SEA) First Team. Back row from left: Ken Jones, Sharon Lynch, Richard Williams. Front row: Mike McManus (capt), Lucy Davis, Brenden Caine-Lee (Paul Woodhouse is missing from the photo).

is the shadow-ghost of the type encountered by Dave Williams at Sandbach Old Hall (see page 66). These are dark, vaguely human, forms which vary in height from 2 ft to 6 ft and move, silently, a foot or two, above the floor or ground.

Then there are the non-visual spirits which express themselves by speaking, moving objects about, producing odours – either foul or sweet – or by some other sensory way. And, it is well-known that the presence of a ghost, visual or not, is often accompanied by a marked fall in temperature.

Another interesting feature of the paranormal is the widely varied length of hauntings, which can range from a single manifestation – if that can be called a haunting – to a span of centuries. Many start abruptly and end equally abruptly. Others just peter out.

In recording the events and incidents published here, I have attempted to include details of time, place, and names, where such information is available.

Finally, I must acknowledge my debt to those folk who helped me with the research for *Haunted Places of Cheshire*, and in particular to the members of the Supernatural Encounters Association (SEA). By allowing me access to their files, a free choice of their photographs, and the generous support of their advice throughout the work of researching and writing the book, the members of the SEA rendered my task significantly easier than it would otherwise have been. I embarked on the research for *Haunted Places of Cheshire* resolved to thank everyone who helped me by name, but it soon became obvious that, were I to do so, I would arrive at the bizarre and impractical situation where the list would rival the main text in length. That being so, I can only express my heartfelt gratitude in general terms to all those who helped me by answering my queries with patience and courtesy.

Jeffrey Pearson

A corner of Godley Green, Hyde, c. 1900, drawn from a faded photograph by David Scott.

•Cheshire•

ALTRINCHAM

Almost certainly, those Altrincham residents who remember the Studio 1 cinema do so because of the haunting. Studio 1 was a small enterprise which shared the former Hippodrome theatre building with a bingo club. The paranormal activity started almost as soon as the cinema opened in 1963. Footsteps were heard by members of the staff in rooms that were known to be empty; doors opened and closed without any human intervention; from time to time, both patrons and members of staff encountered patches of severe cold;

The Hippodrome, about 1920.

and the tip-up seats in the auditorium often snapped down, apparently by themselves. Up in the projection room, projectionists Dave Grant and Philip Drinkwater struggled to cope with projectors that were switched off and on – sometimes half way through a film. The tip-up seats and both projectors were professionally checked and all of them were found to be in good working order.

Inevitably, word of this weird activity soon spread through the town and, equally inevitably, it reached the ears of the media. The situation was featured in a BBC television show, and articles appeared in the local and regional newspapers.

There was much speculation about the cause of the disturbances. Some struggled to find a natural explanation, but there were many who were prepared to believe that the happenings at Studio 1 were of supernatural origin. Séances were held and contact made with a number of spirits, but they all refused to identify themselves. The matter was never satisfactorily resolved, but the most popular theory was that the mischief was the work of the ghost of Edward Hargreaves. Edward was the younger son of Thomas Hargreaves of Rochdale, a former owner of the Hippodrome. Frustrated by his parents' refusal to countenance his ambition to act, Edward hanged himself.

The haunting continued, intermittently, until both the cinema and the bingo club closed in 1983. The old Hippodrome building was demolished in January 1987, and all traces of it were buried under a new office block. So far, there has been no indication that the spirit, or spirits, have moved to the new building.

BIRKENHEAD

Without doubt, the Worsley Arms is haunted. Glasses fall off shelves when there is no-one about, the beer taps in the cellar are occasionally and mysteriously turned off and, from time to time, the temperature in one corner of the bar plummets, a phenomenon that is always accompanied by a sudden stench. Chill and stench persist for two to three minutes. Then there are the cats. Licensees Ken and Sheena Kal have five cats, some of which can occasionally be seen focussing on something invisible to human sight and following its movements with their gaze. Whatever it is, it does not seem to trouble them too much.

So far, however, there has been insufficient evidence to identify the ghostly culprit or culprits. No legend has been retained in folk memory, no apparitions have been seen, and the pub's meagre recorded history offers no clues. In 2001, Supernatural Encounters Association researcher Barry Lowe made a search at Birkenhead central library, and discovered that the first mention of an inn on the site was dated 1885, when the hostelry was called the Queen's Hotel. There are, however, indications that a building – possibly the same one – occupied the

The Worsley Arms at Birkenhead.

Woodside area site in 1855. Barry found some brief references to the pub over the years, and he was able to list the various licensees. He also discovered that it was at some date after 1966 that the pub's name was changed to the Worsley Arms.

There was, therefore, very little background information on which the SEA could base an investigation. Even so, on the night of 23rd/24th September 2001, an SEA team held a night-long vigil in the pub. Disappointingly, the spirit or spirits refused to co-operate. The whole night's work amounted to a few isolated ghostly words picked up on their tape recorders.

In 2002 a group from Liverpool John Moores University held a vigil at the pub, but Ken and Sheena have yet to hear from them. Also in 2002, Granada Television broadcast an item about the hauntings at the Worsley Arms. Despite this widespread interest, by August 2005, when this account was written, the possibility of identifying the spirit(s) seemed as remote as ever. It is a problem common to many – perhaps most – haunted places.

* * * * *

The situation at Riley's Snooker Club, in Argyle Street, is a little clearer. There, investigators had the advantages of starting from the basis of a recorded apparition, and a fragment of folk memory.

Over the years, staff and club members at Riley's have been mystified by a series of strange incidents. Odd, inexplicable, noises are heard and objects are moved. Every evening, after the last customer has left and before the building is closed for the night, a staff member places the red balls in position, inside their wooden triangles, ready for the next day's play. Every morning, the staff find that the triangle on table 10 has been moved; often, it is lying on the floor. There have also been occasions when staff have glimpsed ghostly figures in places where no one should have been. Then, in spring 2005, there was a clear sighting of an apparition. A young member of staff was clearing up after the club had closed for the night when he saw a woman sitting down on some stairs in an area closed to the public. 'He came back to the bar, looking very pale indeed,' recalls club barman, Neil Craven. 'He'd asked her to leave, but she wouldn't. She just sat there. We went back with him, but there was no-one there and no alarms or sensors had been disturbed. It is said that, when the place was a music hall, the owner's wife sat down and lit a cigarette with matches that accidentally set fire to the curtains and she burned to death.'

The sighting of the ghost prompted staff member Jean Courtenay to attempt some research at Birkenhead central library. She discovered that the story of the woman burning to death had some foundation.

Does the ghost of Edith Cole haunt Riley's Snooker Club, Birkenhead?

The snooker club is housed in a converted cinema, which was built in the 1930s on the site of the demolished Theatre Royal. Between 1898 and 1905, the theatre was leased by a W. W. Kelly, whose wife, Edith Cole, was a popular actress. It seems, however, that she was not over-intelligent. She met her death while attempting to clean the long kid gloves she always wore on stage in some highly inflammable spirit and, at the same time, to smoke a cigarette through a long holder. However, the sketchy local records which exist imply that she did not die in Birkenhead at all, but that she died many years after she and her husband had moved elsewhere. The place and date of her death are not recorded locally. Could it be that her shade has made the journey to haunt a spot where she was particularly happy during her lifetime?

In May 2005, a team from the Stockport Club Zero Ghost Group conducted a vigil at Riley's. During the vigil, three members of the group said they had seen shadows moving around the room. Cold spots developed, and spirit orbs were caught on camera. The investigators did not, however, manage to establish direct contact with any of the resident spirits.

Afterwards, team leader Paul Prole said, 'We spent nearly nine hours at the club, and were joined by several members of Riley's staff for the investigation. After an all-night vigil, we now believe that Riley's is a very paranormally active place with several active spirits within its walls. It definitely warrants further investigations into this magnificent building, and we hope to return in the near future.'

BRIMSTAGE

Standing in the centre of the Wirral Peninsula, Brimstage Hall is an ancient place. The original towered house is medieval, with two more wings added in Elizabethan and Victorian times. It is also a place of many mysteries. No records survive to reveal exactly when and for whom it was erected, and those relating to the folk who lived and worked at the house over the centuries are few and fragmented.

Even so, there is evidence enough to suggest that the apparition of a woman dressed in white, which has been seen wandering though the passages at night, is that of Margaret, the youngest daughter of the Earl of Shrewsbury, who, following an unhappy love affair in 1807, committed suicide by throwing herself from the tower.

There are no clues, however, to indicate the identity of another ghost which is said to haunt the hall. All that is known is that she is an elderly woman dressed in black and is sometimes glimpsed in the Victorian wing. She is always seen from the knees upwards because the floor was raised after she died.

Brimstage Hall.

It seems that neither of these ghosts has appeared for many years, and Gerald and Dawn Mallinson, who rented the hall during the 1970s and 1980s, were almost complete sceptics as far as the paranormal was concerned. Almost, but not quite. The curious behaviour of their labrador dog gave them some cause for thought. A normally adventurous creature, the dog steadfastly refused to enter the vaulted chamber at the foot of the tower. Numerous attempts to help him to overcome his fear met with no success. No amount of cajoling or even bribery with favourite tit-bits would induce him to cross the threshold. Instead, he would stand just outside the door with his feet firmly planted on the floor, hackles raised and teeth bared in a snarl. Having tried, but failed, to find a satisfactory explanation for the animal's refusal, the Mallinsons were forced to the conclusion that there must be something very odd about the chamber which only the dog could detect.

Brimstage Hall is no longer a home. The house and its outbuildings have been adapted for commercial purposes, incorporating a restaurant and a shopping complex. If there have been paranormal incidents in recent years they have almost certainly passed unremarked in the bustle of everyday trade.

CHESTER

Chester's supernatural population reflects the 2,000 years of the city's history. The apparitions glimpsed from time to time include Roman soldiers; medieval monks and nuns; at least one cavalier and one roundhead; an 18th-century sailor; and a number of weeping maidens lamenting lost lovers. There is also a sprinkling of unidentifiable, non-materialising, but very active, supernatural spirits.

One of the best-known of Chester's ghosts is that of a monk which haunts the church of St John the Baptist and the surrounding area. Very possibly it has haunted the spot for 1,000 years, but the first recorded sighting in modern times occurred in 1941. A certain Mr Michael Cooper Porter was walking in the church grounds with a young priest when they were approached by an exceptionally tall man dressed in monk's habit with the hood up. There was something frightening about his appearance, and they tried to avoid him by turning away. But to no avail. With amazing speed, the stranger moved to confront them again. He addressed them in civil tones, but in an unfamiliar language. When they responded with gestures to indicate that they could not understand him, he disappeared. They were able to discover that the tongue he had employed was Anglo-Saxon, a language used in England between the 7th and 11th centuries.

The next recorded sighting of the monk occurred in 1973. On 7th December, the *Chester Observer* published a letter from Victor W. Fishbein (of New York) who stated that late at night on the previous

Friday, 30th November, he had been returning to his hotel by way of the cobbled footpath that runs down to the river on the west side of St John's when, suddenly, he was confronted by a tall stranger. The bright moonlight and the footpath lamps enabled him to see that the man was dressed in a monk's habit with the cowl raised. The stranger spoke to him in a guttural language, which Fishbein could not understand. He was certain that it was not German, because he spoke that language fluently. When he told the monk that he could not understand him, the other man seemed to be distressed, and spread his hands out as if pleading for help. Fishbein apologised for not being able to understand him, stepped round the monk, and tried to resume his journey. Then curiosity prompted him to look back. To his amazement, the footpath was empty. There was no sign of the other man. The path is bounded by high walls on both sides, and human flesh and blood could not possibly have reached the distant far end of the path in the few seconds which had elapsed since he had left him.

The cobbled alley beside St John's church, Chester.

The following week the paper printed a response from another correspondent, Chester resident John Sandford, who wrote that he had had a similar experience to Fishbein's the previous summer. 'I was walking home late one night using the same pathway. When I was about halfway down I met a man dressed like a monk, in a black robe and wearing sandals. He spoke to me in some outlandish language which I could not understand, and I said so. He repeated his request, but it was no use. I didn't understand him. The monk seemed saddened and turned away. I proceeded on my way, but after a few steps something made me turn round to have another look at the strange figure, but to my surprise, it had disappeared.'

These three sightings are on record, but it is possible that there have been others which have not been so chronicled.

Inevitably, there are sceptics. Alan Lees, a churchwarden at St John's and currently chairman of the parish church council, has little time for such reports. Over the 45 years that he has worshipped at the church he has yet to hear of anyone mentioning a similar experience. He knows that at choir practice on dark winter evenings a cowled monk may be seen standing in the semi-darkness at the far end of the church, apparently listening to the rehearsal, but he also knows that investigation has long since shown the figure to be no more than a teasing shadow-reflection thrown on to a polished door. It is a trick of the light spilled from the choir stalls!

* * * * *

Chester is well-endowed with ancient inns, almost all with at least one resident ghost – far too many for every one to be considered in a book of this length. However, there are two examples which can be outlined to represent the whole.

The Victoria, in Watergate Street, has traded – under a number of different names – since the 13th century, but there are those who maintain that it has only been haunted since the advent of metal beer barrels in the final quarter of the 20th century.

The pub stands hard against St Peter's church with its cellar built over part of the church crypt. The introduction of the metal barrels brought a change in delivery practice. Instead of the draymen easing them down a ramp, as they had done with the old wooden barrels, they now drop them on to a mattress-type arrangement designed to absorb the force of the impact. It is said that, as the result of a miscalculation, the first metal barrel dropped into the Victoria's cellar carried the mattress and part of the cellar floor down into the crypt. Theorists propose that it was this accident which stirred up a spirit or spirits that had previously been sleeping the years away.

So far (to spring 2006), the haunting has been confined to the mischievous teasing of some members of staff by spirits indulging in such pranks as moving cutlery, glasses, keys and other small items about, or touching folk, or whispering.

The experiences of barmaid Jay Roberts are typical.

'I sometimes feel a hand on my shoulder or back when there's nobody about,' she explains. 'And one morning I was by myself, clearing up before we opened for the day, when I heard a voice call my name. I heard it clearly, but I knew there was nobody else on the ground floor where I was working.'

To date, no apparitions have been seen.

By many standards it is all very mild. Even so, there are those who find it worrying enough.

* * * * *

The Pied Bull in Northgate Street is a residential inn of great character. It can boast ancient beams, a fine 17th-century staircase, and an unusually high level of supernatural activity.

'Particularly in and about rooms eight and nine,' says manageress Lesley Doody. 'And we have regular guests who ask for one of those rooms in the hope that they might see a ghost.' One couple, who stayed in room nine in May 2005, did see a ghost – but not until they developed their photographs. A snap of the wife standing by the huge fireplace showed a bluish misty, human-sized, column standing just slightly behind and to one side of her. Disappointingly, there is nothing in the known history of the inn to suggest just what that particular apparition was, and there is no record of it appearing to anyone else.

The Pied Bull at Chester.

Very different is the case of the Pied Bull's best-known ghost. A certain John Davies met his sudden death at the inn on 27th September 1690, when he fell down the cellar stairs with a knife in his hand. Over the years, members of the pub staff have said that they have felt an icy presence in the cellar, and there are those who are not comfortable working down there.

It is, however, possible that Davies's shade may sometimes desert the cellar for the more comfortable parts of the inn. One long-serving member of staff, who does not wish to be named, believes that she and a colleague once caught a glimpse of him in the former first-floor television lounge – now the haunted room nine. One morning in 1985, they went to clean the room, and saw the figure of a man sitting on one of the chairs. They thought little of it, believing him to be a guest. They looked away, but when the witness glanced back again, a mere heartbeat later, he had vanished. The only fact she remembers about the figure she glimpsed so briefly is that he was wearing a blue and white checked shirt. She has not heard of anyone else encountering Davies.

Occasionally, members of staff or customers feel the touch of a ghostly hand on their shoulder, a ghostly prod in the back, or a sudden, strange, momentary, cold draft. On one (unrecorded) day in 2003, a customer dining at the pub told Lesley Doody that she was a medium, and that she could detect the spirits of two children in the bar. She said that one was a girl aged 12 to 13, and that the other was her brother, a boy of about 10. They had died, she said, of starvation.

COMBERMERE ABBEY

C ombermere Abbey was the setting for one of the best-known of all ghost photographs. Today a (quiet) holiday centre and tourist attraction, the abbey stands between Nantwich and Whitchurch, just on the Cheshire side of the county boundary.

Founded as a Cistercian monastery in 1133, after the 1540 Dissolution, the abbey passed into the hands of Sir George Cotton, vice-chamberlain to the household of Prince Edward (later Edward VI). Cotton built himself a fine manor house on the former abbey lands, and his descendents continued to live there for the next four centuries. In 1817, Sir Stapleton Cotton was created viscount and took the title of 'Lord Combermere'.

Legend holds that, at one time, the abbey was haunted by the ghost of a little girl whose appearance foretold the death of a family member. An account of the haunting appeared in the December 1870 issue of the magazine *All the Year Round*.

'Miss P-, niece of (the second) Lord Combermere, often stayed at the abbey before her marriage. One evening, Miss P- was alone dressing for a very late dinner, and as she arose from her toilet glass to get some article of dress, she saw standing near her bed, a little iron one placed out in the room, away from the wall, the figure of a little girl dressed in a very quaint frock, with an odd little ruff round its neck. For some moments Miss P- stood still and stared, wondering how this strange little creature could have entered her room.

'The full glare of the candle was upon its face and, as she stood looking at it, the child began to run round the bed in a wild distressed way, with a look of suffering in its little face. Miss P- still more and more surprised, walked up to the bed and stretched out her hand, when the child vanished, how or where she did not see, but apparently into the floor. She went at once to Lady Combermere's room and inquired of her to whom the little girl she had seen in her room could belong, expressing her belief that she was supernatural, and describing her odd dress and troubled face. The ladies went down to dinner for many guests were staying in the house. Lady Combermere thought and thought over this strange appearance. At last she remembered that (the first) Lord Combermere had told her that one of his earliest recollections was the grief he had felt at the death of a little sister, of whom he was very fond, at four years old. The two children had been playing together in the nursery, running round and round the bed overnight. In the morning, he was told she had died in the night, and he was taken by one of the nursery maids to see her laid out on her little bed in the coved saloon.

'The sheet placed over her was removed to show her face. The horror he felt at the first sight of death made so vivid an impression on him that in extreme old age he still recalled it. The dress and face of the child as described by Miss P- agreed precisely with his remembrance of his sister.

Both Lady Combermere and Miss P- related this to the writer.'

Whether the ghost-child appeared to predict the second Lord Combermere's death in November 1891, when he was struck by a horse-drawn carriage, is not now known, but it was his ghost which is the accidental subject of the famous photograph. Taken in the abbey library on 5th December 1891, while his lordship's funeral was in progress four miles away at Wrenbury, the print shows the faint figure of a man sitting in a high-backed chair.

The photograph was taken by a visitor, Sybil Corbet, who had decided to photograph the very fine, panelled, abbey library instead of attending the funeral. She settled on a time exposure of an hour, set the camera, and went for a walk. She had no reason to suspect that, when

The photograph which is claimed to show the ghost of Wellington Stapleton Cotton, 2nd Viscount Combermere: it was taken on 5th December 1891 while his funeral was in progress four miles away. The print shows the faint figure of a man sitting in the high-backed chair on the left.

the plate was processed, it would show anything other than her intended subject of the room, its books, and its furnishings. Although not all parts of the ghostly figure were equally visible, the face was clear enough for the 3rd Viscount to recognise his father.

There is, however, no record of the 2nd Viscount's shade making a second visit. The little ghost-girl, too, seems to have departed. Indeed, for the last 115 years the abbey appears to have been free of all further paranormal activity.

In 1917 the 4th viscount sold the estate to Sir Kenneth Crossley, founder of the bus and car manufacturing company. 'I've never been troubled by ghosts,' declares Sarah Callander Becket, Sir Kenneth's granddaughter, and present owner of the estate, 'and, as far as I know, neither has any member of my family.' Even so, she agreed to a request from a large paranormal group to hold a vigil at the abbey on the night of Friday 30th September to Saturday 1st October 2005. The group left on the Saturday in a state of high excitement after promising to send Mrs Becket a copy of their report in the course of the following four weeks. Unhappily, despite a number of reminders from Mrs Becket, at the time of writing this account (eight months later), she is still waiting for it.

CONGLETON

If a certain Lady Warburton had not managed a sort of survival as a ghost, Congleton would have forgotten her long ago. Even Robert Head's well-respected *Congleton, Past and Present* (1887) makes no mention of her.

As it is, just three main facts about the noble lady have been retained in local folk memory: that she lived at the, now-demolished, Hulme Walfield House, that she lived in the early part of the 19th century, and that she died a sudden death. On the actual manner of her death, however, there is some disagreement. There are those who say that, following an unhappy love affair, she threw herself from an upstairs window on to a cobbled yard, while others maintain she was killed by a sash window which fell on her neck as she was leaning through it.

Whatever the facts of the matter, over the years her shade has continued to remind the town of her former existence by strolling on the short footpath between Rood Hill and the site where her house once stood. Indeed, so many sightings have been claimed that the path has long since become known as 'Lady Warburton's Walk'.

* * * * *

No one, it seems, can recall when any of the Lion and Bell's apparitions last made an appearance. Certainly it has not been since 2003, when the present licensee, Julian Harris moved in. If, that is, one discounts an occasion when Julian glimpsed a ghostly leg.

One morning, in early 2005, he came downstairs just before the pub opened, not realising that the bar manager, Mandy Frost, had arrived. The unexpected sight of her sitting behind the bar, quietly eating her lunch gave him a start – much to Mandy's amusement. The following morning he thought he saw an opportunity to gain his revenge when he spotted the back of a trousered leg sticking out from behind a supporting post. Assuming Mandy was standing on the other side of the post, he crept silently up on the leg and jumped out onto the spot where Mandy should have been standing. Only to find there was no one there, and that the leg had disappeared.

It would have been surprising if the Lion and Bell were not haunted. An 18th-century coaching inn, it has seen many generations of customers pass through its doors. To suppose that a few spirits from such a mighty throng might choose to return seems more than likely. There may, perhaps, be some paranormal links to the facts that, in the early years of the pub's existence, a customer hanged himself from the inn sign; and that an area at the immediate back of the building, now occupied by a dance floor extension was, for a long time, the site of an undertaker's parlour.

The Lion & Bell at Congleton.

From all reports, the pub would seem to be haunted by a rich assortment of ghosts and spirits. All manner of unidentified shades, it is said, flit about the top (second) floor, an area now used for storage. Certain it is that none of the staff or customers is happy to go up there. Not that the ground floor has been spectre-free. Before Julian's time, two apparitions were seen by both customers and staff in the bar area. One was the ghost of an apron-wearing little old lady, who wore her hair in a bun, and the other was that of a headless man.

While no apparition has been seen for at least three years, there are indications enough that many of the pub spirits remain active. 'Sometimes, when the place is closed and I'm working quietly by myself,' explains Julian's daughter, Emily, 'I can hear whispering when there's nobody about. And sometimes, I see a movement from the corner of my eye, but when I turn my head there's nothing there.'

CREWE

On 22nd January 1996, *The Crewe Chronicle* reported the story of a collie's deliverance from paranormal torment. It was a sudden change in the dog's behaviour which had alerted its owners to the fact that something was troubling it. One morning, at three o'clock, the couple – who do not wish to be identified – were woken by their dog barking frantically downstairs. It was a startling departure from his normal, placid, behaviour. Until that morning, the animal, named Bob, had slept peacefully through the nights. Alarmed, the husband went downstairs to investigate. He found the house secure and Bob apparently barking at thin air. The same thing happened the following morning, and on successive mornings. Always at 3 am. It was puzzling and disturbing. The owners could see that something was troubling the animal but they were at a loss to guess what that something might be.

Eventually, they mentioned this odd behaviour to a friend, Lesley Shepherd, who also happens to be a medium. Lesley suggested that the problem could be of supernatural origin. She investigated and made contact with the spirits of two children who had lived in the cottage 100 years previously. They told her that their family had been large and poverty-stricken, and that they had died of starvation. They said that they liked returning to their former home and that they had only been teasing Bob for fun.

Lesley told them that, although they were welcome to visit the house, they should not torment the dog. With the situation explained to them, they expressed their regret and undertook not to tease the animal again. After that, Bob and his owners were once more able to sleep undisturbed throughout the night. The dog died, peacefully, in 2003.

It is possible that the spirit children still visit the cottage, but they have yet to be seen or heard by the householders.

* * * * *

Another success recorded in Lesley's bulging case-book concerns a haunted massage parlour. In early 2003, the desperate proprietor of the Crewe business appealed to her for help. The place, she said, was haunted by the ghost of a snarling, hefty, red-haired woman, dressed in Victorian clothes. The apparition had been glimpsed from time to time by both customers and members of staff but, more often, she asserted her presence by making strange, unpleasant, noises or throwing objects about or hiding them. The situation was unnerving both the staff and the customers, and undermining trade.

Lesley visited the converted, three-storey, terraced house accompanied by two student mediums, and prevailed on the ghostly virago to make an appearance. 'She was' recalls Lesley 'spitting fire and brimstone'.

The apparition was enraged but Lesley managed to calm her sufficiently to discover the reason for her fury. In broad Irish tones, she declared that she was a good Catholic woman and that she was outraged by the activities that were taking place under her roof.

When Lesley was eventually allowed to speak, she explained that time had moved on. She told the apparition that the house was no longer hers, so she should not distress herself over the activities that were going on there. She also suggested that the spirit should make her way to the other side, where she rightly belonged.

Reassured by the medium's words, the ghost left for the spirit world through a tunnel of light.

DISLEY

A Disley phenomenon, still held by some to be the work of supernatural forces, is more easily explained away than many others. A carved stone standing at the side of the hilly and lonely Whaley Bridge to Disley road bears the inscription, 'William Wood. Eyam, Derbyshire. Here murdered July 16th AD 1823. Prepare to meet thy God'.

The facts of the case are documented in the Chester Assize records. Wood, a cattle dealer, was returning home from market with his pockets jingling when he was attacked by three robbers. Two escaped but the third, Joseph Dale, was caught and hanged at Boughton, Chester, on 21st April 1824.

It is, however, the existence of a slight hollow in the ground close to the stone which has prompted the creation of the supernatural legend. It is a depression which never fills up nor does anything grow there. From time to time, attempts have been made to fill it up and to plant grass on the patch, but to no avail. On every occasion the earth and stones and grass seeds used have soon – sometimes overnight – been found mysteriously scattered about the surrounding area, leaving the hollow empty again.

Local tradition holds that this hollow was created by Wood's head as his attackers smashed it into the earth during the attack, and that some supernatural power has ordained that it shall remain barren for all eternity as a perpetual denunciation of the horrible murder committed there.

Prosaic minds, however, maintain a more plausible explanation. They point out that the ground at that spot lies below the level of the road, and argue that it is almost certainly water washing off the carriageway which accounts for the barren hollow. That being so, it probably existed, unremarked, long before the murder.

DUDDON

The macabre name of the Headless Woman pub, at the village of Duddon, is a reference to an incident which occurred during the English Civil War. Warned that a patrol of Roundhead troops were on the way to arrest him as a Royalist, Squire Joseph Hockenhull hid the family treasure and fled with his wife and children and most of his servants. He left only his housekeeper, Grace Trigg, behind in charge of Hockenhull Hall, thinking that the soldiers would not harm her.

In that he was mistaken. Frustrated in their search for loot, the Roundheads proceeded to torture Grace in an attempt to make her reveal where the valuables were hidden. To no avail. Despite the pain, she refused to betray her master's trust. Finally, infuriated by her silence, the soldiers cut off her head.

Throughout the centuries that have since passed, it is said that Grace Trigg's ghost can still sometimes be seen, carrying her head under her arm and walking along the old bridle path between Hockenhull Hall and the spot where it meets the Tarporley Road, near to the pub.

For some years, a carved figure of a decapitated woman holding her head stood in the pub garden. Originally a ship's figurehead, it was stolen at some unrecorded date in the past. Folk memory recalls that the head disappeared first, followed, a few weeks later, by the body.

It is many years since anyone claimed to have encountered the headless ghost, but there is no doubt that the pub and its surroundings are haunted. Strange shadows flicker on the ceilings, odd, inexplicable, bumps and bangs are heard, sudden cold spots occur, and customers who stand drinking in the front passageway are sometimes jostled by an invisible elbow.

A team from the Supernatural Encounters Association held a vigil and séance at the Headless Woman on the night of 26th/27th February 2005. They came to the conclusion that the pub is haunted by at least six spirits: five ghosts of folk who died in the 17th century, and a sixth

The Headless Woman, Duddon.

of an elderly man who died of a heart attack at the pub in 1943.

A particularly weird incident occurred on the night of Wednesday, 24th August 2005. Just after closing time – at about 10.45 pm - two customers left the pub by the back door, intending to make their way round to the car park, where a lift awaited them. Suddenly, one of the men spotted a dark figure striding down the old bridle path towards them. By the light spilling out from the pub windows, he had the impression of a tall figure in a grey jacket. 'Good night,' he called. There was no reply. The figure bustled on past them and disappeared into a six-foot-high garden wall. 'Did you see that?' the witness gasped, only to discover that his friend had seen nothing.

They went back into the pub. The witness was trembling and deathly cold, and it was minutes before he could manage to tell the story. He had, he said, been a customer at the Headless Woman for 40 years but he had never before endured such an experience. Landlord Gareth Houghton recalls that the witness was still suffering from shock a week later.

ELLESMERE PORT

The Boat Museum at Ellesmere Port is based on the redundant Shropshire Union Canal tidal basin. It was a place where, for some 150 years, goods were transhipped between canal boats and the seagoing vessels that visited the Mersey. In its 19th-century heyday, it was the commercial heart of the town, but the advent of the railways and modern road transport brought decline and finally closure in 1968. Today, thanks to the vision and dedicated work of an army of volunteers, the docks, locks and buildings of the former transport complex have been adapted and re-modelled to create a major waterways museum. Opened in 1976, it is a place of exhibitions, archives, conferences and festivals. All celebrating the country's waterways – past and present.

In October 1995, and, again, in January, February, and December 1998, well-known north-west psychic investigator Mike McManus led teams of observers in overnight vigils at the museum's island warehouse to investigate reports that it was haunted. A huge two-storey building, housing a number of exhibitions, a shop and a lecture theatre, the former grain warehouse was said to be patrolled by the ghost of one Arthur Jones, a night watchman at the canal basin in the 1950s. Unfortunately, nothing more is known about Jones because all the basin's records were lost after it was closed.

As soon as the group entered the building, at 8.30 pm on 14th October 1995, the team medium claimed that she could see the ghostly image of a man in a flat cap, donkey jacket and worn dark trousers. Arthur Jones himself?

After Mike had finished a short briefing, the members moved to their allotted individual observation points. Later, at the de-briefing, each of them said that, while doing so, he/she felt a sense of being followed by an unseen presence. During the vigil some members encountered sudden cold spots, and some caught the occasional strong odours of creosote, sulphur, and soap. From time to time, all members heard the occasional, unmistakable, sound of a door slamming, after they had previously fastened all the doors in the building shut.

The most dramatic incident of the night occurred at 2.26 am when, clearly witnessed by Mike, some invisible force hurled a team member against a plate glass panel, a distance of some six feet. Unsurprisingly, the man was traumatised. He clambered to his feet, shaking and with tears running down his face. After a few minutes he did manage to calm down sufficiently to resume making observations, but the experience was to

The Boat Museum at Ellesmere Port.

have a permanent effect on him. Bravely, he attended one more vigil but in such a state of apprehension that he decided it would be his last.

When they reviewed the events of the night the team agreed that Arthur Jones's ghost was indeed haunting the old warehouse, and that he very obviously resented their intrusion on to what he regarded as his patch.

The vigils held in January and February 1998 were comparatively quiet events, with paranormal activity limited to a few odd noises and smells. The December 1998 investigation, however, proved to be far more rewarding. During the vigil, the eight members of the group heard heavy footsteps above them on the first floor at a time when they knew they were the only people in the building. They also heard occasional, inexplicable, bangs and bumps and caught the same odours they had recorded during the 1995 vigil. At one point Mike McManus was walking past an exhibition boat when its raised sail shivered in the still air. Much more exciting, however, were the apparitions. Three misty, seemingly male silhouettes, were simultaneously glimpsed by the whole group and later one member saw the figure of a man wearing a flat cap, donkey jacket and dark trousers – a description which coincided with that of the spectre recorded on the October 1995 vigil. While it seems reasonable to suppose again that the spectre with the flat cap was that of Arthur Jones, there have been no suggestions about the possible identities of the misty three.

FRODSHAM

There is a shop in Frodsham, located in a converted large Victorian terrace house, where the staff are being subjected to frequent paranormal experiences. The business part of the shop occupies an area which, it is thought, was once the front two rooms while, behind a connecting door on the far wall, a large, covered, storage area occupies most of what was the back room and back yard. There is also a covered passageway running along the side of this storage area. In the shop, the counter stands to the immediate left of the door, as customers enter, and at right angles to it.

Shirley Webb, who was manager from 1999 to 2004, recalls how none of her four assistants – all women – would open the shop up until one of her colleagues had arrived to afford her the courage of their company. Some said there were moments when they saw movements from the corner of their eye, but when they looked there was nothing to be seen, and some claimed to have sensed a presence close to them at times when they happened to be working a little apart from the others.

Shirley had been inclined to give their fears small credence until one winter evening in 2000. The shop stays open until seven and, on that particular evening, Shirley was working alone after her assistants had left for the day. Head bent over some paperwork, she was aware of a man entering the shop and walking past her. She looked up at his back and just had time to note that he was wearing an overcoat and trilby before he turned to his left and disappeared into the wall. Shocked and amazed, she plucked up the courage to inspect the place where he had vanished and found only the solid wall she had expected to find. Next day, she made some enquiries and discovered that there had once been a door where the figure had disappeared. Reluctantly, she found herself obliged to agree that the shop was indeed haunted.

If Shirley had experienced any lingering doubts – if she had considered the possibility that she might have hallucinated that evening – she soon had the reassurance of an expert opinion. From time to time, when she needed extra help in the shop, she called on a friend, Christine Hamlett, who happens to be a rescue medium (see the entries for Northwich and Winsford). On three occasions, Christine saw the ghost of a woman walking along the back passageway.

'She was dressed in a grey Edwardian-type dress, with her hair in a bun. It was obviously a working-type dress,' she recalls. 'On two of the three occasions, she was carrying pies on a tray. And, no, I didn't speak to her. I didn't want to disturb her. She was living in her own time.'

Some research unearthed the fact that there had been a period when the building had housed a butcher's shop.

Hilary Radcliffe, who was one of Shirley's assistants, recalled a weird incident on an occasion when she was working alone in the storage area. 'The doors were all closed,' she said, 'and it was very quiet. Suddenly, I heard a man's voice say, "Morning, love". I looked about, but there was no sign of anyone else in the place. It was unnerving, I can tell you!'

And still the supernatural incidents continue.

Hilary now owns the business. One Sunday, just before Christmas 2005, a day when she was working alone, she briefly left the shop to attend to some matter in the storage area. When she returned she saw a woman standing in the shop with her back to her and apparently looking at the display in the window from the inside. She remembers that the seemingly-potential customer wore a headscarf and a brown coat.

'Can I help you?' Hilary asked, as she turned to fasten the connecting door behind her. She turned back, a second or two later, to find there was no sign of the other woman. Not only that, there had been no sound of the shop door opening and closing. She rushed to the door and looked up and down the street, only to find it deserted.

One day, two or three weeks later, an assistant, Sandra McCleary, was working by herself. Suddenly, at a moment when there no customers in the shop, the door between the storage area and the shop swung quietly open, remained open for a few seconds and then, equally quietly, closed. All without any sign of human intervention. When Sandra summoned the courage to investigate the back area, she found no one there and all the outside doors locked.

To date, no serious attempt has been made to identify the ghosts. The shop staff are of the opinion that they must be the spirits of some of the folk who have lived and worked in the building over the years. But why this particular shop? Why not in every other old Frodsham building?

* * * * *

By way of a contrast to the brisk pace of paranormal activity at that shop, haunting at the Ring o' Bells in the Frodsham suburb of Overton is very slow-burning. In fact, during her 30 or so years as landlady, Shirley Wroughton-Craig has seen the ghost just once. Furthermore, there has been no other evidence of paranormal activity in the form of doors opening by themselves, objects moving apparently of their own accord, strange indoor mists, and so on. Which would seem to amount to a clear case of dereliction of duty. A 17th-century building standing on a site which has been occupied since at least *Domesday* (1086), would seem to deserve rather more diligence and effort from its resident shade.

It was early one morning in the 1980s that Shirley saw the ghost. She woke in semi-darkness and immediately sensed that something was wrong. Her Siamese cat, which always slept on the bed, was standing, tensed and staring at something to one side of the room. As Shirley's eyes adjusted to the poor light, she made out the figure of a nun standing by a cupboard. She immediately realised that she was looking at a ghost, but she was not alarmed. Instead, she watched with interest to see what

The Ring o' Bells, Frodsham.

her unexpected visitor would do, and she experienced a pang of disappointment when the spectre merely proceeded to fade away.

She switched on the light and saw that it was four o' clock. She was absolutely certain that she had not dreamt the incident and, as a teetotaller, she knew she was not suffering from the effects of over-indulgence. Then there was the cat. The cat was still on its feet, glaring at the spot where the apparition had stood, with its fur fluffed up and its tail like a lavatory brush.

No one had warned Shirley that the pub was haunted before she took it over. Neither she nor those folk to whom she mentioned the incident had heard of the ghost. That being so, she had no alternative but to regard it as an isolated, inexplicable, incident. Until, that is, two or three years later when a local historian, who called in the course of some unconnected research, told her that the pub is reputed to be haunted by the ghost of a nun. Shirley's informant did not, however, know who the nun was or when she lived or why her shade should haunt the Ring o' Bells. Those facts all seem to have been lost in the mists of time.

GAWSWORTH

Mary Fitton.

There are some who have come to believe that Mary Fitton has finally deserted Gawsworth. For over three centuries her ghost haunted the village, making not infrequent appearances at the Old Hall and the (now old) rectory, in the church, and in the lanes. Appearances which came to an almost abrupt end about 50 years ago.

For centuries, Mary's parental home, the attractive Old Hall, was the seat of the Fitton family. Mary became a lady-in-

Gawsworth Old Hall, former home of Mary Fitton.

waiting to Queen Elizabeth I at the age of 17, but she was dismissed when the queen learnt of her adulterous relationship with William Herbert – later the Earl of Pembroke. Herbert was sent to the Fleet Prison for the offence.

Mary Fitton died in 1647, in her 70th year, at Harefield, Middlesex, after she had been married and widowed twice and produced two legitimate and three illegitimate children.

Her will stipulated that she should be buried at Gawsworth, but there is no record of her burial either there or at Harefield. Even so, wherever Mary Fitton's mortal remains were laid, there have been witnesses enough to testify that her ghost returned to her native village. For example, Abraham Holland, a former sexton who died in 1917, said that he often saw her while he was oiling the lamps for Sunday services. There would be a rustling of silk followed by a low sigh, and from behind the altar came Mary, dressed in a green riding habit. Glancing from left to right at her ancestors' tombs, she would glide down the chancel and then disappear into the vestry. The church would go very cold.

Those who regard Mary's possible departure with regret should not, however, abandon hope. They could well take heart from the Swettenham experience (*qv*).

HELSBY

W hen Mrs Ann Jones heard that I was researching material for a book, she related to me the following account which happened in the early hours of 29th August 2001.

She was driving along the A56 back to her Frodsham home after attending a wedding at Chester and it was, she says, an experience she will never forget. A widow in her mid-fifties, she had good reason to hope for a trouble-free journey. It was a clear, moonlit night, and there was very little traffic to share the road with her. Then, about a mile from Helsby, Ann felt her Fiesta lurch. Sensing immediately that she had a puncture, she stopped the car. It was irritating, but she was not too troubled: she had a mobile phone and she was a member of the AA. She climbed out and closed the car door behind her. She inspected her tyres and discovered, as she had thought, that the nearside back tyre was punctured. She called the AA, and received an assurance that a patrol man would be with her in 15 minutes. That done, she looked about her at the moonlit landscape of fields and hedges in which she had stopped. The nearest houses were half a mile behind her at the village of Dunham-on-the-Hill. She was alone, but she was not alarmed: the road was quiet, the roadside lamps were still lit, and the air was warm. All that being so, she decided to wait on the roadside footpath.

After a few minutes, she saw a distant figure making its way towards her from the direction of Helsby. At first, she thought it was a woman because it appeared to be wearing a white dress but, as it drew nearer, she realised it was advancing with a very masculine sort of stride. Her initial surprise turned to uneasiness. She climbed back into the car and locked the doors. As the figure continued to walk towards her she saw that it was, indeed, a man wearing what she recognised to be an old-fashioned working smock. His bearded face was half-hidden by the brim of his hat and he carried some sort of tool – perhaps an adze or a rake – on his shoulder. There was something very strange about him.

As fear clutched at her, Ann shrank down on her seat in an attempt to render herself inconspicuous. The walker reached the car and passed it, staring into the distance. He went by in complete silence. There was no sound of footfalls.

Breathing a little easier, Ann pushed herself into her normal sitting position and looked in her driving mirror. There was no sign of the man. She turned on her seat to look directly through the rear window. Still she could not see him. It seemed that he had vanished. Even so, she determined not to get out of the car until she saw the lights of the AA vehicle. She found she was sweating and shaking.

The AA man arrived a few minutes later from the direction of Dunham-on-the-Hill – the direction towards which the strange figure seemed to be walking. But the AA man said, no, he had not seen a man dressed in a smock and carrying something on his shoulder. In fact, he had seen no-one during the whole of his seven-mile journey from Chester.

He listened carefully to Ann's story. When she had finished, he nodded. 'Seems you've seen a ghost,' he remarked. 'I've heard a couple of tales like that over the years.'

'Is this road haunted, then?' Ann asked.

'Could be,' replied the other, 'or it could have been just a one-off. I've never heard tell that it's haunted. The tales I've heard have all been to do with other roads, but it does seem to be typical of the sort of sighting other folk have had.'

HYDE

A farmhouse at Godley Green, on the outskirts of Hyde, was the setting for a haunting that troubled a series of tenants for nearly 80 years.

It began about 1830, when a servant claimed that she had seen the figure of an old woman pass through her room in the dead of night. At first her report was treated with scepticism but, when the whole household started to hear mysterious footsteps walking through rooms and up and down the stairs, doors opening and closing, apparently of their own accord, pots and pans rattling and tumbling to the floor, and bedclothes being snatched away from sleepers, disbelief turned to fear.

Enquiries among the neighbours brought the information that the last survivor of the previous tenant family had been an old witch-like woman and, with it, the inference that it was her spirit that was causing the mischief.

The efforts of the Reverend James Brooks, pastor of Hyde Chapel, to exorcise the spirit by praying and reading the Bible at the house, met with only limited success. The visitations became less frequent, but they still occurred from time to time.

One day in 1890, the members of the then tenant family – parents and four half-grown children - were startled to hear a rumbling sort of noise coming from a bedroom overhead. When they investigated, they were met by the sight of an old rocking chair violently going back and forth as if some particularly energetic but invisible person were seated in it. The rumbling noise was caused by the rockers working on the bare floorboards. The farmer and children were seized with terror but, made of sterner stuff, the wife stilled the chair by just sitting on it.

What seems to have been the end of the hauntings was marked by a particularly weird pair of incidents. One windless day in 1906 the tenant's wife was hurrying home to her brother who was lying sick at the farm, when a high blackthorn hedge on one side of the lane suddenly started to thrash about. Realising immediately that there could be no natural reason for the phenomenon, she was filled with a sense of foreboding. A moment later, her fears were heightened, when an old woman dressed in white – a stranger – appeared from the direction of the farm. The farmer's wife hurried on, but she arrived home too late. Her brother, she learned, had just died.

The house is still occupied, but there have been no reports of supernatural activity there for a hundred years.

KELSALL

I n mid-2005, new owners transformed Kelsall's Royal Oak from a traditional, English inn into a modern restaurant-pub, renamed The Oak. The change appears to have stunned the building's apparently numerous ghosts. The amount of paranormal activity, which had previously verged on the exuberant, plummeted.

Among the apparitions which appeared before the transformation was that of a thin, gaunt-looking male, dressed in modern clothes, which was seen from time to time by both members of staff and customers standing at the bar. Graham Hawthorne, the last landlord before the pub changed hands, saw one female ghost in Victorian clothing and, on a later occasion he came face to face with a different female ghost with a half-grown female ghost child. Also, strange shadows were sometimes seen moving about in the cellar.

The Oak public house was formerly called the Royal Oak.

Then there were the spirits that did not appear, but asserted their presence in other ways. On the ground floor, doors opened and closed without any human intervention; stacked stools were mysteriously unstacked; footsteps were heard in rooms that were known to be empty; and, occasionally, the loudspeaker was turned on when the speaker cabinet was locked. Upstairs, too, there was much paranormal activity. Chamber maids making the double bed in room 4 often sensed a presence on the opposite side of the bed and, occasionally, they would turn from some other task to find the imprint of a body lying on the bed they had just made. Some guests asked to be moved from room 5 because they sensed an unseen presence in the room with them. In the private quarters, landlady Rachael Hawthorne's mother always left her room locked with the windows closed when she went out, but she often returned to find her windows open.

Living with such a high level of paranormal activity, Graham and Rachael readily agreed to a proposed investigation by the Supernatural Encounters Association.

The SEA held their first vigil on 16th October 2004, and the second on 6th November 2004. They photographed orbs, both in the main house and in the outbuildings and, by means of séances, they were able to identify three of the resident ghosts. Two were the shades of a woman named Annabel and her child, Jane – almost certainly the woman/child shades already seen by Graham. Annabel told the researchers that she had owned eight dogs and had been hanged by the villagers as a witch. The team was not able to discover how Jane had died. The male ghost, it emerged, was the shade of Robert Jameson, a landlord of the Royal Oak in the early years of the 20th century.

The slump in paranormal activity which accompanied the conversion of the building and the business has continued to the time of writing – some eight months later. Perhaps all the noise and change prompted some of the spirits to leave. It is, however, equally possible that there may yet be at least one paranormal presence at the Oak – a few of the cleaners are still uneasy when they are working in some of the bedrooms.

KNUTSFORD

I n 1996 a sickening stench of boiling meat drifted through the newly-opened Booths supermarket at Knutsford. Occurring intermittently and lasting on some occasions for minutes and on others for the better part of an hour, it was at its most pungent in the warehouse.

Almost certainly, it deterred a number of customers and it certainly prompted consternation among the management. Intense searches were conducted throughout the building in an attempt to find the source of the nuisance, without success.

During the course of town-wide discussion and speculation prompted by the problem, a local historian, who does not wish to be identified, recalled that the supermarket had been built on part of the site occupied by the county prison until 1915, and that the jail records included entries to the effect that there had been many complaints, from both prisoners and townsfolk, about the stench of the beef that was boiled in the prison kitchen on Wednesdays and Sundays.

Booths supermarket, Knutsford.

And the stench was not the only problem for the supermarket. Staff members glimpsed weird shadows flitting about the warehouse; and odd, unaccountable, bumps and bangs were heard throughout the building. Strangest of the noises was the occasional sound of whistling. Piercing and tuneless, it originated in odd corners or from behind stacked bales, but prompt investigation always failed to locate a culprit. Infuriatingly, the whistling always stopped a heartbeat before the searcher came in sight of the spot concerned. It was the same local historian who observed that whistling had been forbidden in the prison, and that surreptitious whistling had often been used frequently by convicts employed on work details to goad the warders.

Could it be, asked some folk, that the supermarket was experiencing some sort of paranormal time ripple?

Whatever the cause, happily for the company, the phenomenon was short-lived. Both stench and noises gradually petered out over the course of the first six months of the store's existence.

* * * * *

A second, much older, ghost story is firmly lodged in Knutsford legend. It seems that, at some unrecorded date in the early 19th century, at a time close to midnight, a turnpike keeper on the Knutsford to Chelford road opened his gate for three men travelling in a gig. As the vehicle passed, he saw that two of the men appeared to be supporting a young man who was sitting between them.

The following day, the young man's body was found lying at the side of the road near Ollerton. He was not known locally and he carried nothing which might help the local constable to identify him, but his good clothes and his smooth hands spoke of some status. The manor court retained his clothes as evidence for many years, but his identity was never discovered.

Henry Green's account of the incident in his *History of Knutsford* (1869), prompted an astonishing response.

Writing in *Cheshire Notes and Queries* for 1889, one Albert A. Birchenough expressed his amazement at the Green story. He recounted how one calm, starry, night in October 1872 he had been walking along the same road to Chelford, when he heard the rattling sound of a horse-drawn 'conveyance' behind him. He moved over with the intention of asking for a lift, but the vehicle seemed to stop some twenty yards short of him. He heard voices and the sound of two or three folk jumping down.

He turned and walked back to ask for the lift, but found there was nothing there. No vehicle, and no passengers. As he looked about him, he saw another walker approaching. He accosted the newcomer and explained the reason for his bewilderment, but the other could suggest no possible explanation.

The recollection remained a puzzle until he came across Green's book, some 20 years later.

LYMM

I t would have been surprising if the Dingle Hotel had not been haunted. A 17th-century timber-framed building, it stood on a site which had been occupied by a previous building from Norman times. Thirty generations had lived and worked and died on the spot. Small wonder, then, that at the general acceptance in Lymm, at least one spirit had haunted the place.

Until 1929 the building had served as the parish rectory. Then, judged to be too big for modern needs, it was sold. For the next 30 years or so, it was successively adapted for use in a number of roles, including tea-rooms and a sports club, before it was bought by an entrepreneur. The new owner re-furnished the old rectory and, in 1960, he opened it as the Dingle Hotel.

From the launch of the new business, both guests and members of staff began to experience the sort of weird phenomena which local tradition

The Dingle Hotel in Lymm was demolished in 1997.

had long associated with the place. Small objects such as pens, keys, coins, and spectacles disappeared and reappeared later in improbable places, and doors opened and closed without human intervention. Local historian Joe Griffiths has a vivid recollection of a particularly hair-raising incident. Together with a friend, Dave Pownall, he was engaged in repairing some of the building's under-floor pipe-work, when they reached a spot immediately outside a bedroom door. To avoid the possibility of a guest stepping out of the room and into a cavity, they checked with the receptionist that the room was not in use before they raised the floorboards. She assured them on the point and, when they tried the door, they found it to be locked. But, hardly had they started work, than the locked room's television and radio blared into life. Startled, they called on the receptionist to unlock the door. When she did so they found the radio and television set to be on, but the room to be unoccupied – at least by the living. The radio and television were both tested and found to be in perfect working order.

Occasionally, the ghost of an old lady dressed in grey was briefly glimpsed sitting in a corner of the hotel, but no folk memory existed to suggest her identity.

The hotel closed in the mid-1990s, and the building was demolished in 1997. A small housing development now occupies the site. So far there have been no reports of paranormal activity in any of the new houses (but see the entry for Sale in this book).

MACCLESFIELD

The Bate Hall is the oldest pub in Macclesfield. It was founded in the early 16th century, and is a place of oak beams, panels and settles, and can also boast a fine Jacobean staircase and a priest's hole. The Bate is haunted, most notably by the apparition of a young woman in a long grey dress. She is, however, a somewhat shy spectre. There seems to be no record of when she was last seen, although there is general agreement that it was many years ago.

Even so, there is no lack of paranormal activity at the pub. Doors have been known to open and close without human intervention, and spirit orbs sometimes appear on photographs taken in the bars. On one occasion, cellarman Norman Davies was mysteriously locked in the kitchen when the pub was closed and he was the only living person in the building.

In April 2005, landlord Nick Rockcliffe gave the north-west-based Pathfinders Paranormal Investigators permission to hold an overnight vigil at the Bate. Group leader Paul Jowett recalls that, during the course of the vigil, the group medium managed to contact the ghostly young woman, thereby ending a certain amount of speculation that she might have departed for the other side. The ghost explained that she had met her death after she had been accused of witchcraft. Pursued by a lynch mob, she had tried to escape by seeking refuge in the Bate, but she had

The Bate Hall, Macclesfield.

found no sympathy there and, instead, the occupants hanged her from a banister. Unfortunately, the medium was not able to establish the ghost's former name or a date for the murder or whether she planned to materialise again.

NANTWICH

Like Chester, Nantwich is a town where there are too many haunted places for them all to be mentioned, and just two of them are recorded here.

Churche's Mansion stands at the point where Hospital Street meets the town's London Road. A fine, half-timbered place, it was built as a house by local merchant Richard Churche in 1577. Over the centuries it has been used for a variety of purposes, including a cow-keeper's store.

There is no way of knowing when the first ghost moved in, but Churche's Mansion was certainly well haunted during the last 30 years of the 20th century when it was adapted for use as a restaurant. Cutlery moved, crockery fell off tables and on to the floor, and lights were switched on and off – all without any sort of human intervention.

And then there were the apparitions.

On one occasion during a wedding reception, two bridesmaids who were climbing the stairs passed two girls descending the stairs who were dressed in a manner which made them think they were also bridesmaids but from another wedding. When they returned to the ground floor they looked about, but they could see no sign of the other girls or any evidence of another wedding party. They mentioned their observations to the bride, who asked the proprietor whether another wedding party would be sharing the restaurant with her own. He assured her that no

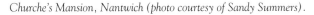

Churche's Mansion, Nantwich (photo courtesy of Sandy Summers).

such booking had been made. Told of the mysterious girls on the stairs he said, 'They must have been a couple of our ghosts.'

One December evening in the late 1970s, the Skinner family of Neston were celebrating son Richard's birthday with a dinner at Churche's Mansion. They had all finished the main course when Richard and his cousin, Pam, felt someone arrive behind them. Thinking it was the waitress wanting to clear the used plates, they both leaned outwards. To Richard's amazement, a man walked between them, continued straight through the table, and disappeared into the wall. The sighting lasted for no more than three or four seconds, but that was time enough for him to see that the ghost was wearing 17th-century style dress of a black tunic, white cuffs and a white square lace collar. Its face was hidden by long black hair which fell down at the sides.

This column of light caught on camera at Churche's Mansion, Nantwich, was identified as an angel by Sandy Summers.

No one else in the party saw the ghost. Like Richard, Pam had sensed a presence behind them, but she had not seen the spectre. She had, however, felt a sudden chill sweep over her as it passed. Richard's father, who was sitting almost opposite him, said that he had experienced an eerie feeling of time standing still. No one else in the party had noticed anything unusual.

They mentioned the incident to the waitress. She was not surprised. 'Yes, well, we're having some repair work done on the building at present,' she commented, somewhat dismissively, 'and that always makes the spirits restless.'

In 2001 the restaurant was closed, and in the following year the building changed hands. The new owner, Sandy Summers, is a psychic and an angel therapist (that is one who is skilled in helping others to communicate with their guardian angels). Even before she took possession of the building Ms Summers established that there were three ghosts in residence: a civil war cavalier, a girl from the following century, and William Churche, father of the man who built Churche's Mansion. (Possibly by that time the ghost seen by Richard Skinner and the ghostly 'bridesmaids' had found their own way to the other side.) As a trained psychic, Ms Summers helped the cavalier and the girl over to the other side, but William Churche's ghost chose to stay. He is still there, and Ms Summers often has long conversations with him. At the time of writing, however, she has yet to see him.

* * * * *

When Nigel and Jane Hobson acquired the tenancy of the Victorian Railway Hotel in 1993, they were unaware that it was haunted. They were left to learn about their supernatural guests from personal experience.

It did not take long. The family – the Hobsons have four daughters – soon began to feel the sudden cold spots that occur about the place, to realise that the small objects which occasionally disappear from their private quarters – pens, keys, coasters, and the like – usually re-appear a day or so later, and that stools stacked for the night in the bar are sometimes found to be unstacked by the following morning. And they all sensed the brooding presence which lurks on the main hotel staircase.

It was about two months after they moved into the hotel that Jane first saw an apparition. The Hobsons always sleep with their bedroom door open to allow them to hear any untoward sound in the hotel. One night Jane awoke and, by the subdued glow of the hotel's emergency lighting spilling into the room from the landing, she saw a half-grown

The Railway Hotel, Nantwich.

girl standing in the doorway. She wore, Jane recalls, a loose white-cotton nightdress-looking garment. Thinking one of her four daughters was sleep-walking, Jane slipped out of bed. As soon as she moved, the girl turned and walked away. Jane followed her along the passage, but lost sight of her when she turned a corner. When Jane turned the same corner the girl was nowhere to seen. She checked on her daughters and found them all to be asleep.

Three or four months after that, Jane went into the Hobsons' private lounge and saw three small children huddled together on the floor by the fireplace. She just had time to note that they were wearing plain loose clothes before they disappeared.

Those sightings all took place in the Hobsons' private quarters. Just one apparition has been seen in the public areas of the Railway Hotel, but it does return from time to time. Described as the figure of a pale-faced old man, wearing a mackintosh and a bowler hat, he stands in a corner of the bar. He has been seen by both members of staff and customers but, in the way of these things, some can see him while others cannot. Not that he lingers – one moment he's there, and the next he's gone.

A team from the Supernatural Encounters Association held a vigil at the hotel on the night of 26th/27th October 2002. In the glow of the emergency lighting, their camcorder caught a small, blue, light floating about near the bottom of the stairs. They were also able to photograph a strange white mist which appeared on the stairs and lay there for some five to ten seconds. Unlike a terrestrial mist, it did not slowly gather and then gradually melt away. In an appearance typical of paranormal mists, it appeared fully formed and disappeared in an instant.

The strange mist photographed on the stairs of the Railway Hotel, Nantwich, on 27th October 2002, by SEA member Paul Woodhouse.

The team conducted a séance, and identified two of the resident ghosts as being those of Walter Jones, a landlord of the hotel during the 1940s, and Fred Roberts, a former engine driver.

One of the strangest incidents experienced by Jane and Nigel occurred in May 2004. They decided that, as their oldest daughter Katie was 22 and very competent, they would take a rare holiday in the form of a week cruising on the Llangollen canal, leaving Katie in charge of the hotel. Their plan was to make haste to reach Llangollen, and then cruise back in a leisurely manner. They set off on a Saturday and reached Llangollen on the Monday.

On Monday night Jane could not settle in bed. She felt as if she were burning. She got out and walked up and down. It was a cold night, but she still felt hot. Nigel urged her to return to bed with a warning that she would catch a chill, but she just could not do so. Suddenly, the telephone rang. It was Katie calling to tell them that the hotel was on fire. The blaze turned out to be serious enough to close the hotel for six weeks, but fortunately no-one lost their life. The fire service investigated the incident but were unable to reach a satisfactory conclusion about the cause of the fire. They offered one or two tentative theories, but nothing conclusive.

Jane believes that her feelings of discomfort on the boat could well have been a paranormal warning of the fire.

NORTHWICH

For years it has been well-known throughout Northwich that the Roebuck inn is haunted. Occasionally, strange noises – bangs and scrapings inexplicable except in terms of the paranormal – were heard; brief cold spots were experienced in various parts of the building; members of staff sometimes sensed a presence standing close to them when they had thought they were alone; and the shadow of a woman was occasionally glimpsed on the ground floor.

The Roebuck in Northwich is haunted by the ghost of a former landlady.

Then, quite suddenly, in early 1997, the paranormal incidents became markedly more frequent. Overnight, chairs were found to have been mysteriously stacked and pictures thrown to the floor. Much more unsettling were the appearances of a shadow, seen clearly on a number of occasions by both customers and members of staff, gliding from the front door to the bar. Some customers were able to shrug off the experience, but others became fearful, and trade started to suffer. The problem became so serious that licensees Sue and Tony Salter contacted rescue mediums (and sisters-in-law) Christine Hamlett and Jackie Dennison in the hope of finding a solution.

Jackie and Christine responded by visiting the Roebuck on a number of occasions during the summer of 1997 and, with the aid of their spirit guides, succeeded in contacting the spirit responsible. She told them that,

Northwich-based rescue mediums Jackie Dennison (left) and Christine Hamlett.

during her earthly life, her name had been Hannah Latham, and that she had once owned the pub. Her strolls about the place, she explained, are made to check on the state of the business. If she does not like the landlords or disapproves of something she expresses her displeasure by creating problems. She is not trapped at the pub, but she likes to visit regularly. When Jackie and Christine explained that her appearances were having an adverse effect on trade, she agreed to reduce them.

Jackie did some follow-up research at Northwich library, and discovered that a Hannah Latham had, indeed, been a part-owner of the Roebuck in the mid-19th century. She had owned the pub jointly with her first husband, Joseph Holland, from 1853 until his death in 1860. She remained as sole owner until she remarried William Latham in 1861. She and Latham were joint owners until her death on 6th March 1876, at the age of 55.

After Jackie and Christine's intervention, there was a reduction in paranormal occurrences at the Roebuck but, from time to time, signs of an increase in Hannah's activities oblige them to make return visits.

RUNCORN

During the late summer and autumn of 1952, reports of some spectacularly malicious paranormal activity drew the attention of the national media to the (then) small industrial town of Runcorn. Unfortunately, the most widely-consulted contemporary summary of the affair leaves something to be desired. Written in the form of a pamphlet by Richard Whittington-Egan, and housed at Runcorn library, it is marred by a number of inconsistencies and omissions that render any attempt to reach a satisfactory assessment of the episode difficult.

According to W-E, the strange disturbances started in a bedroom at 1 Byron Street on Sunday, 10th August, where 17-year-old John Glynn and his 68-year-old grandfather, Sam Jones, were sleeping. The spirit signalled its arrival by scratching loudly in a dressing table drawer. In the days and weeks that followed it became increasingly violent, throwing small objects such as a clock and books across the room, and tilting heavier items of furniture, like the dressing table and a blanket chest. Much of this activity was accompanied by a loud hammering.

News of the haunting soon attracted the attention of the local and then the national media. Knots of journalists and of everyday curious folk collected in Byron Street. For some reason, the police became involved. They investigated, and declared they could find no evidence of trickery. After a well-known spiritualist of the time, Phil France, had held a three-hour séance in the room, he announced that there was definitely a poltergeist present. The Reverend W H Stevens, the local Methodist Minister and a member of the Society for Psychical Research, also conducted an investigation and came to the same conclusion.

Whittington-Egan called at the little house about seven weeks after the disturbances started. There was still, he noted, a number of curious folk standing about in the street. As an interested writer, W-E secured permission to spend the night observing events in the bedroom.

No 1 Byron Street, Runcorn.

He examined the room carefully before John Glynn and his friend, John Berry, retired to the double bed for the night. He found no evidence of trick devices, so the boys clambered into bed and W-E switched off the light. Almost immediately, a crash came from the dressing table and, a moment later, an alarm clock flew across the room. 'That's it!' exclaimed Glynn. During the hours which followed all manner of similar incidents occurred, but W-E noticed that there was a marked change in the pattern of disturbances when he started to patrol the room with his torch at the ready. The spirit seemed to become less sure of itself. There were long pauses when W-E stopped close to the bed. At one point, a sudden probing ray from his torch caught John Glynn's arm rapidly withdrawing from the direction of a 'spirit knock'. It also occurred to W-E that all the alleged phenomena which had taken place that night, could easily have been engineered from the bed. He asked the boys for permission to tie their hands and feet, but they refused. He also states, somewhat confusingly, that he was not allowed to remove all possible accomplices from the room, without previously having mentioned that a fourth party might have been present.

Even so, and almost incredibly, he left the house still prepared to believe that some sort of phenomena existed. It is difficult to accept his explanation that he did so because the pattern of disturbances at Byron Street was typical of poltergeist hauntings.

W-E records that, at about the same time that the disturbances began at Byron Street, three pedigree pigs belonging to a Mr Crowther of Pool Farm, Runcorn, died for no apparent reason and, within a fortnight, all 53 of his pigs were dead. Five veterinary surgeons examined the bodies, but were unable to account for the animals' deaths.

Two days after his last pig died, Crowther was astonished to see what he described to W-E as a large black cloud about seven feet high, shapeless apart from two prongs sticking out from the bottom, advancing straight down his yard. In his account W-E fails to state where its advance ended, but he did say that Crowther told no-one at the time! His wife was obviously not so uncommunicative because, three days later, she told him she had seen the cloud in the yard. A few weeks after that, it attacked Crowther in his kitchen, with its prongs seeking his throat. It disappeared when he switched the light on.

In the meantime the disturbances had been continuing at Byron Street. Shortly after Crowther fought the cloud off, his assistant, Sam Jones, arrived at the farm with the urgent request that he should go to the house in Byron Street. There, according to W-E, Crowther saw the forked cloud hovering above John Glynn's bed. Sadly, the author does not mention who had sent Jones for the farmer, or what happened after Crowther had grasped the situation.

The farmer saw the cloud for the last time on 13th December 1952, seconds after he had released his two dogs from a shed. The animals rushed past him barking frenziedly. He turned and saw the cloud. It was smaller and lighter in colour than on previous occasions and moving along the ground. The dogs pursued it, snarling and snapping, until it escaped by rising into the air and disintegrating.

It was also in December 1952 that the disturbances came to an end at 1 Byron Street.

Of course, a report which begs so many questions did not entirely confound the sceptics. And, after the 50 or so years which have passed since the disturbances recorded by Whittington-Egan came to an end, nothing of a similar nature has occurred at Runcorn. The town, it seems, is now spirit-free.

SALE

Possibly it is the fact that wealthy cotton-trade heiress Hannah Beswick remained unburied for some 110 years after her death which renders her spirit restless. For more than two and a half centuries her ghost has made appearances in one or other of the widely-separated towns of Sale in Cheshire, and Oldham in Lancashire.

Hers is a strange story. Folk memory holds that Miss Hannah Beswick of Birchen Bower Manor, in Holinwood, Oldham, was obsessed with a fear of being buried alive. In an attempt to forestall that possibility, she left very specific instructions in her will that her physician and executor, Dr Charles White, was to ensure that her body was embalmed and kept above ground for 100 years. A further condition, the story goes, specified that, together with two other witnesses, he was to inspect the body every year. In return for these services Hannah left White the whole of her estate.

Hannah Beswick died in 1757 and, still according to folk memory, the good doctor proceeded to carry out his obligations under the terms of the will. He embalmed the body in tar and swathed it in heavy bandages, leaving only the face uncovered. That done, he placed the body inside a long-case (grandfather) clock. Curtains were fitted across the clock glass, and every year they were drawn back, and the mummy was solemnly inspected by White and two other witnesses for signs of life.

That Miss Beswick's corpse was mummified, placed in the long-case clock and examined annually is beyond question, but detailed research conducted in the early 20th century revealed that the reason given by Charles White for keeping the body above ground was a wily fabrication. An examination of Hannah Beswick's will revealed that it contains no mention of embalming and, as for legacies, it specifies a payment of just £100 to Dr White for his services, together with a sum of £400 to defray funeral expenses.

The researchers discovered that the lie was the basis of an imaginative scheme conceived by White to ensure the continued existence of what he considered to be an important local enterprise and to stave off personal financial ruin. During the early 18th century, Charles White and a financier, Joseph Bankcroft, entered into a partnership with the object of founding an infirmary at Manchester. Because the very considerable sums which they each invested in the project fell short of the total capital needed to launch it, they borrowed £25,000 – a vast sum in those days – from Hannah Beswick.

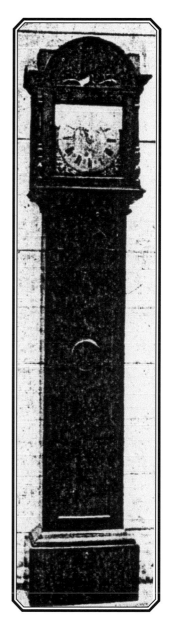

The long-case clock which held the mummified body of Lady Beswick for more than 100 years.

*A contemporary engraving of
Dr Charles White.*

The infirmary was built and staffed, and the first patients admitted.

Then both White and the infirmary project suffered a severe blow, in the shape of Bankcroft's death. The withdrawal of Bankcroft's investment in the infirmary by his beneficiaries and the loss of his financial acumen placed a heavy extra burden on White's shoulders. When Hannah Beswick died two years later, he found himself faced with destitution and his infirmary project with destruction. If all the beneficiaries of Hannah Beswick's will had been able to claim their inheritance, as a debtor of her estate he would have been forced to raise what funds he could from the sale of the infirmary property and from his own resources.

He overcame the threat by misusing his position as Hannah's physician. He seems to have seized the will as soon as she died, and before anyone else could see it. Then falsely claiming that he was her sole executor and knowing that, as the law stood at the time, a will could not be read until the deceased was buried, White lied that Miss Beswick had specified that her body should be preserved above ground for a hundred years after her death.

Just how he managed to maintain the ruse until his own death, 56 years later, is now a mystery, but maintain it he did.

When White retired he moved from his Manchester home to Sale Priory taking Hannah's corpse with him – presumably to avoid the

WHITE, Chalres

C.C.C. Abstract of the Will dated 25th July 1757 of Hannah Beswick of Cheetwood, Lanc. Spinster.

First all debts and funeral expenses &c. to be paid then gives to John Whittaker Strangeways Co. Lancs, Gent. £200
To Charles White of Manchester Co. Lanc. Chyrurgeon £100
To Margaret daughter of Thomas Gorton of Salford Co. Lanc. Chapman £50
To Hannah wife of John Wilson of Ainsworth Co. Lanc. Chapman £50 and her gold wa: and chain.
To Ann wife of said Thomas Gorton her silver waiter in case it be not taken for ; her brocaded silk night gown and all her Brussels Lace
To Elizabeth Wood of Manchester spinster one silver meat spoon marked H.B. and a of silver candlesticks but if she be dead then to said Ann Gorton or her represei
All the rest of her silver plate unto Esther Robinson daughter of her cousin Thon Robinson of Salford.
To Mary Greame of Salford spinster her brown silk negligée and petticoat.
All the rest of her wearing apparel together with the half part of her household and the whole of the linen yearne and flax unmanufactured to the said Esther Robi also £100 and two chests of Drawers &c and her Grandmother's picture &c &c
To Ann Robinson another daughter of the said Thomas the other half of her househo linen &c and an oak chest of drawers &c but if she dye before 21 years then the s siad Esther Robinson and her representatives
Also gives to said John Whittaker and Charles White £200 in trust that they or th survivors shall place the same out at interest and pay the same to Sarah Jenkinsoi Manchester spinster during her life and at her heath to dispose of the same equal: amongst Ann, Peter and Joshua daughter and sons of the said Thomas Robinson
Also gives to said John Whittaker and Charles White £300 in trust that they or th survivors &c place the same aout at interest for the use of Ann, Peter and Joshua Robinson daughter and sons of said Thomas when they attain 21 years respectively (amongst them.
Also gives to said John Whittaker and Charles White £290 in trust that they or the survivors shall take £130 out of same and bind Thomas son of her cousin Thomas Rok clerk to some reputable attorney when he arrives at the proper age.
Also to take out of the £290 two further sums of £30 and £30 and therewith bind re apprentice John and Peter sons of said Thomas Robinson to some good jointer and wi remaining £100 to bind apprentice Joshua Robinson youngest son of the said Thomas think fit.
Also gives to her Executrixes £400 in order to defray the expenses of her funeral there be any over plus to dispose of the same discretionally amongst her Father's relations without giving account to any person for all or any part.
Also mentions a messuage situate in King Street in Manchester which she gives to si Esther Robinson during her life and after her decease she gives the same to John Robinson son of the said Thomas his heirs and assigns for ever.
Also mentions two several messuages lands &c with their appurtences situate in ; Chappell-en-le-frith Co. Derby called by the names of Hall Hill and Dig Leach now (in the tenure of Mary Ford widow her assigns which she gives to her cousin John Hac the Elder of Cradingbrook Co. Chester his heirs and assigns for ever.
Also mentions copyhold messuages &c situate in Bradford in tenure of William Cloug which she gives to Edmund Besswick of Blakeley and Ann his wife during their joint and after their death or death of their survivors, then to Ann Ogden of Blakeley an heirs forever.
Also gives all that her messuage &c lands &c situate in Chadderton Co. Lanc. comonl by the name of Claytons now or late in the tenure of Joshua Collison, and also her cottages with appurtences in Chadderton callded Bradley Bent late in tenure of Geoi Lawton and John Whitehead, also all that her messuage situate in Chadderton known b;

possibility of someone else activating the will by burying it. After his death, in 1813, the mummy passed, under the terms of his will, to a Dr Richard Oliver. Oliver, in his turn, bequeathed it to the Museum of the Manchester Natural History Society in Peter Street, Manchester. There it was exhibited from about 1828 until, the dissolution of the Society in 1868.

Hannah Beswick was, finally, buried in an unmarked grave in Harpurhey Cemetery, Manchester, on 22nd July 1868.

Her ghost has appeared to many witnesses over the years – both before and after her burial. Most of these appearances have been in the Oldham area, but there have been enough at Sale for locals to claim that her ghost haunts the former Priory estate. The house itself was demolished in 1923 but parts of the grounds, including Priory Wood, remain undeveloped. From time to time, walkers swear that they have caught glimpses of a woman dressed in 18th-century clothes among the trees in the wood. After prompt searches found no one in the vicinity at the time, the general conclusion was that the sightings were of Hannah's shade.

Almost certainly, some sightings – and even hauntings – remain unreported in the local press, such as the experiences recounted to local historian Alan Morrison by a woman who lives in a house on Dane Road which borders the former Priory estate. She told Alan that one night during the 1960s, when she was heavily pregnant with her first child, she woke in the small hours to see a strange woman sitting in a rocking chair at the foot of the bed. The ghost, who seemed to be in her sixties, wore a lace shawl and cap, and she was knitting. The witness was terrified. Even so, she managed to retain enough self-control to shake her husband awake, but when they looked back the strange woman had gone. The witness had no doubt that her visitor had been the ghost of Hannah Beswick.

The same thing happened the following night, and every succeeding night during the remainder of her pregnancy. On several occasions the witness managed to rouse her husband when the apparition was still clearly visible to her, but he could never see it. She was convinced that

Hannah was knitting for the coming baby, so she soon lost her fear. The appearances ended after the baby – a daughter – was born. There was no repetition of the haunting during her second (and final) pregnancy. Twenty years later, in a letter sent while at university, the older girl told her mother about a kind old lady who sat in a rocking chair and talked to her and played with her when she was small.

There is something of a postscript to the Hannah Beswick saga. It seems that, throughout, the displaced clock works were carefully maintained and travelled with the case and the mummy. After Miss Beswick's long-delayed funeral, works and case were re-united and, at some unrecorded date, the clock passed into private hands.

In June 1972 the local Sale newspaper reported that the (unnamed) owner wished to be rid of it. So much so that he offered it to some relatives, but they refused to have it in their house. He then submitted the clock for sale at auction. In recording that it was bought by Neston man, Gordon Hare, for £252, a reporter probably found much joy in the opportunity to describe it as a 'grand*mummy* clock'.

SANDBACH

A team of investigators from 'Ghost Haunted, North-East' which conducted a séance at Sandbach's Old Hall Hotel on the night of 25th/26th September 2003, came to the conclusion that it was haunted by at least fourteen spirits. The figure did not surprise Sue Hall. Even before she bought the hotel in 1996 she had known it to be haunted, and learned of some of the individual ghosts. It was, however, not until she moved in that she came to realise just how active many of them were. Small incidents – sudden brief falls in temperature or items of cutlery moved – are commonplace, and few weeks pass without the occurrence of some memorable, supernatural, happening. Happenings like the occasion in June 2005 when a shadowy, vaguely human form suddenly reared up in the hallway in front of

The Old Hall Hotel, Sandbach, is one of the most haunted buildings in Cheshire.

general assistant Dave Williams. About 5 ft 6 ins in height, it moved silently along the hallway and disappeared through the closed door of the ladies' toilets – an experience which instantly converted Dave from a sceptic to a firm believer. Anecdotes of that sort are legion. Small wonder it is, then, that the hotel has become a place of pilgrimage for ghost hunters from all parts of the country.

A splendid example of timber-framed construction, the hall was built in 1656 by lord of the manor, Sir John Ratcliffe, on the site of an earlier hall which was destroyed by fire. That fire is believed to linger on in a strange phenomenon connected with the double bed in room 11. From time to time, guests leap out of bed in the middle of the night convinced that the room is on fire. Once on their feet, they look about and see that there is no sign of fire. Everything about the room looks perfectly normal, as does in fact the bed.

Among the many apparitions that have been seen is that of Sir John Ratcliffe himself. A tall figure in 17th-century dress, he is unmistakable. Sue has come face-to-face with him four times since she bought the hotel and, on every occasion, she was so taken aback that she was unable to react positively in the fleeting moment he was visible. Other ghosts include an old lady who is sometimes glimpsed sitting by the bed in room 11; two girls, aged about 12, said to have been prostitutes, who are seen and heard in various parts of the building; a bee keeper who is sometimes glimpsed in her protective clothing walking from the front door to the stairs; and a spectre known as 'the grey lady'. It is said that some of the panelling for the hotel was brought to the Old Hall at Sandbach from the nearby Haslington Hall. When it was removed the workmen found, concealed behind it, the skeleton of a baby. It is thought that the grey lady is the child's mother, who moved with the panelling and continues her pitiful, endless search for her baby at Sandbach. There is also a ghostly dog seen occasionally in room 1, and a ghostly ginger cat that Sue has spotted at different locations about the building.

Then there are a number of spirits which never materialise, but make their presence felt in a variety of other ways. There have been far too many manifestations of supernatural activity at Sandbach Old Hall to record all of them here, but the following three examples are typical.

In 2000, Sue engaged a firm of contractors to repair the east gable end of the building. During the course of the three months that the project occupied, the workmen were continually harassed by spirits. Their radios were switched on and off, their tools were moved, and sometimes hidden, and they were assailed by noises with no visible sources, such as footfalls and giggling. By the time the work had been completed they had been reduced to a state of near-distraction.

Possibly it was the same spirits who tormented one of the chefs. He, too, was taunted by inexplicable sounds and frequently discovered that his utensils had been hidden. Often he would tidy his knives away at the end of the day, only to find them arranged neatly in order on his work table the following morning.

Room 11 at the Old Hall Hotel, Sandbach.

Matters came to a head one evening in 2001. During a confrontation between the chef and Sue in the kitchen, Sue raised her voice at one point. As soon as she did so, she felt a hand on her shoulder and a loud voice say, 'Ssh!' Startled, she looked at the chef. 'Did you hear that?'

'Hear it!' he exploded. 'I [expletive deleted] hear that sort of thing all the time.' And he promptly handed in his notice. Interestingly, his successor has never been subjected to the same sort of harassment.

One evening in January 2005 while Sue was sitting at the bar, a glass panelled internal door clicked open. It opened rather like a door with a faulty catch – except the catch was not faulty. Sue stood up, crossed the floor, and closed it. A little later, it opened again. Again, she closed it. This sequence occurred a number of times before she gave the door an extra sharp pull, in the hope that it would shut it properly. As she started to return to her stool she saw that barman Dave Williams was looking past her, wide-eyed with astonishment. She swung round just in time to see the image of a woman silhouetted on the glass panel of the door before it disappeared. She rushed back and snatched the door open, only to find that the corridor on the other side was completely empty.

With its impressive cast of shades and high level of supernatural activity, there is good reason to believe that the Old Hall Hotel at Sandbach must be of the most haunted buildings in Britain.

SAUGHALL

When Carl and Helen Jones assumed the management of the 14th-century Greyhound Inn at the Wirral village of Great Saughall in 2002, they had no idea that it was haunted. The first indications they had of supernatural activity were the mysterious noises – thumps and bumps – which they occasionally heard

The Greyhound Inn, Great Saughall.

when the pub was closed. These, however, they could dismiss as the sort of noises that old buildings are liable to make as their fabrics adjust to changes in temperature.

Far more difficult to ignore was the claim made by one of the two cleaners that she had been grabbed by the shoulders while hoovering in the passage. She turned, but could see no-one. From time to time over the following months, she was subjected to similar assaults which confirmed – at least to her satisfaction – that she had not been mistaken and that her assailant was a ghost.

The other cleaner was never molested in that way but, in early 2004, she saw a ghost. She was working behind the bar when, suddenly, she realised that she had company, in the person of a man of 19th-century appearance. He sported a heavy beard and wore a long black coat and waistcoat, with a watch-chain. He was occupied in attempting to draw himself a pint, and, although he looked solid enough, she realised he must be an apparition. Her reaction was nothing less than magnificent. 'Clear off, you cheeky bugger!' she shouted, and the ghost promptly disappeared.

One evening, also in early 2004, Carl and two barmaids were sitting chatting in the lounge after closing time, when they heard the clatter of furniture from the empty bar. They investigated and discovered that some of the bar stools, which they had stacked only moments previously, were lying on the floor. They were certain that it was not a case of careless stacking because they had stacked those same stools on countless previous occasions without their falling over.

On the night of 24th/25th April 2004, a five-strong team from the Supernatural Encounters Association conducted a vigil at the Greyhound. They set up their standard equipment of night vision camcorder, thermometers and audio equipment in the bar, lounge and passage leading to the gents' toilet. Then they spread about the area and, with digital cameras to hand, they settled down to wait.

When a half-an-hour's patience brought no sign of supernatural activity, chairman Mike McManus decided they should try holding a

Equipment is in place at the Greyhound Inn, Great Saughall, ready for the SEA vigil. Note the spirit orbs on the right-hand curtain and on the top left, near the ceiling.

séance in the lounge. They sat round a table, arranged a set of alphabet cards around its top edge, and stood an upturned glass in the centre. Then they each placed a finger on the glass. Almost immediately, team medium Paula Roscoe was able to establish contact with a number of spirits. They included that of a little girl called Aimee, and those of three men, Robert, James and Andrew. The team discovered that Robert was particularly assertive, and that there was friction between him and the other spirits. At one point, Mike McManus asked Robert for a sign to prove that he was, indeed, present. A few seconds later, the team heard the sound of something falling to the floor in the bar. Mike left the circle to investigate, and found that a sign which had been on the bar wall, warning that it was illegal for children to stand at the bar, was lying on the floor.

The other members then joined him. They all saw that the sign had been stuck to the wall with blue-tack. Mike picked it up and pressed it back on to the wall. When he tried to pull it off again, he found the blue-tack was so tenacious that it needed three attempts before it could be dislodged. Jonathan Grady and Paul Woodhouse tried the same experiment, and had similar difficulty. The team agreed, therefore, that it could not have been a failure of the blue-tack which caused the notice to fall.

When Mike examined the recorded results the following day, he discovered that both the camcorder tape and the digital camera memory card had captured a number of orbs, and the audio tapes had caught the spirits' voices and the sound of the bar-notice falling.

Lately, the level of ghostly activity at the Greyhound has fallen to a low ebb. The cleaners who had been involved in supernatural encounters have both left, and their replacements have yet to experience anything of the same kind. Apart from the mysterious-seeming noises, which may have mundane origins, nothing untoward has occurred. Strangely, despite all the evidence, both Carl and Helen Jones remain sceptical about the existence of their ghostly lodgers.

STOCKPORT

Staircase House stands close to Stockport town centre. Built in 1460, the former merchant's house takes its unusual name from the rare cage newel staircase which was installed there in 1618. Behind its disappointing brick façade, there stands a timber framed building of great historical importance.

For almost five centuries, Staircase House served as a home, most notably for the wealthy Shallcross family which occupied it from 1605 to 1730. After the last occupants left in the 1940s, it was adapted to serve a number of casual short-term purposes, until the late Mrs Gwineth Williams established a café there in 1960.

For a long time, Staircase House had the reputation of being haunted, so perhaps Mrs Williams and some of her assistants were not too surprised when they caught occasional glimpses of a ghostly young man dressed in Edwardian clothes on the stairs. Or, rather, half a young man because only that part of the wraith from the waist upwards was ever seen. Unfortunately, as happens in so many cases, the sightings were so fleeting that they precluded any meaningful reaction on the part of the observers. The staff also seem to have accepted an abundance of inexplicable noises and strange, moving shadows as part of the building's character.

In spite of a damaging fire in 1989, the café survived until an even more damaging fire in 1995. The second conflagration caused such extensive damage that there was talk of demolition, an idea that caused widespread outrage and protests throughout the town. Faced with such an outcry, Stockport Metropolitan Borough acquired the house by means of a compulsory purchase order, with a view to restoring it and opening it as a visitor attraction. A £2.4 million grant from the Heritage Lottery Fund provided a sound financial basis for the scheme, but ten years' intensive work was also needed to realise the project.

There is no record of the spirits harassing the workmen, but they lost no time in asserting their presence as soon as the house was opened to the public in August 2005. Within days, members of staff and visitors were reporting odd, apparently

The ghost of a young man has been seen on the staircase at Staircase House, Stockport.

The restored 15th-century bed chamber in Staircase House.

inexplicable, noises, strange moving shadows and, from one staff member, a glimpse of a ghostly figure. So numerous were these reports that on Friday, 2nd September, the Dreamscope Television Company investigated them in a three-hour, night-time, live broadcast. It proved to be an incident-packed occasion. When the three presenters, Yvette Fielding, Derek Acorah and Carl Beattie, began to contact the spirits, the house became suddenly loud with the sounds of tapping, thumping and knocking. Spirit medium Acorah said he heard the names of Robert Wild, Robert Oulton and Thomas Shallcross, all of whom had either owned or lived in Staircase House between the 17th and 19th centuries. At one point the ghost of Thomas Shallcross took possession of Acorah's body, and his ranting was such that a cameraman collapsed and the whole crew later confessed to feeling sick with terror. During the broadcast, a number of viewers rang the station to say they could see ghostly figures moving about the house. One claimed that he could identify a shade he spotted mounting the stairs as that of Robert Oulton, a steward to the Shallcross family in the late 17th century. There was, however, no sign of Mrs Williams's young man.

The broadcast brought a spate of enquiries from ghost-hunting groups and individuals but, for administrative reasons, the borough has decided to allow no more vigils at Staircase House for the foreseeable future.

Some members of staff and some visitors continue to claim they have had psychic experiences, but they are far outnumbered by the sceptics.

* * * * *

Now a suburb of Stockport, the village of Offerton stands to the south of the River Goyt on the site of an ancient north-south roadway and a ford. The road no longer exists and the ford is no longer used, but evidence enough of the old route has been unearthed in the form of laid stones leading down to the river and beyond. It seems likely that the road linked up with the Roman road that crosses the hill called Werneth Low in an east-west direction.

Without doubt, over the centuries Offerton will have seen thousands of travellers making their way through the village in one direction or the other. Detachments of Roman soldiers, perhaps, marching to suppress some disturbance; carriers with their wagons full of coal or timber or some other necessity; pedlars with their trays of household and personal chattels; pilgrims on their holy journeys; masons humping their bags of tools, in search of work; fugitives and their pursuers; rogues and honest men. With such a cavalcade funnelled through the village, it would be strange, indeed, if a ghost or two had not been left behind to testify to its passing.

Such an idea would seem to be supported by the experiences which a resident related to local historian Ray Preston. The witness has lived in Offerton all her life, and in her present Victorian house overlooking the

A likeness of the Romano-British ghost seen at Offerton, Stockport.

Goyt valley and river for many years. Excavations revealed that the house is built on a stretch of the old road.

One mid-morning in 1985, the witness was cutting up apples for a pie. Her three-year-old son, Harold, was standing on a stool and picking up the odd piece of apple and eating it. The witness knew there was no one else in the house but, suddenly, she sensed a presence behind her. She turned, looked towards the open door into the hallway, and saw a tall man dressed in the fashion of a prosperous Romano-Briton, with a cloak held by a large brooch at the shoulder. Thinking that she was hallucinating, and not wishing to alarm Harold, she turned back to her work. When she looked again, two or three minutes later, there was no sign of the man. She was preparing to settle for her original theory of hallucination, when Harold asked, 'Mummy, who was that man?'

Five years later, the witness saw the ghost again. She was sitting in her lounge, knitting, when she looked up through the open door and saw the Romano-Briton standing in the hallway and smiling at her. Before she could recover her wits, he turned and melted into the wall.

SWETTENHAM

The appearance of a ghostly nun at the Swettenham Arms in November 2005 has provided a talking point for the whole village of Swettenham. Was it the return of a ghost thought to have been helped over to the other side in the 1950s or was it the materialisation of a previously unknown spirit?

For centuries Swettenham was haunted by the shade of a nun. She was most often seen about the rectory and the church, and was also occasionally glimpsed wandering around the lanes. Folk memory says that she had been murdered because she broke her vows and married, but it does not retain a record of her name or the date of her death.

Writing in 1951, a former rector, Rev Frank Rider stated that he had seen the ghost in the rectory, and that he knew of three or four other people who had seen it. He also mentioned the 'strong psychic influence' that was present in the rectory when he and his family moved in. Rider took the situation in hand by reciting what he describes as 'absolution' every evening for two weeks. At the time, the measure

The Swettenham Arms.

Frances Cunningham, proprietor of the Swettenham Arms, re-enacts the moment in November 2005 when the ghostly nun appeared.

appeared to be successful because the 'psychic influence' dispersed and the ghost was not seen again.

Unless, of course, it was she who appeared in the Swettenham Arms on 15th November 2005. The ghostly incident occurred towards the end of the lunch-time session, when just one couple remained in the dining room. Suddenly, the wife became aware of a nun standing by the fireplace. She looked very sad and, curiously, she appeared to be standing on stairs where there are no stairs. Before she vanished, the nun told the woman that her name was Sarah and that she was aged thirty-five.

The witness's husband, who had heard and seen nothing, was

astonished when his distraught wife leapt to her feet and hurried out of the pub. She telephoned the local rector, Chris Kemp, for help. Chris told her that he, too, had seen ghosts and suggested that she should speak to Frances Cunningham, joint proprietor, with her husband Jim, of the Swettenham Arms. Frances told her that, as far as she knew, there had been no previous sightings of the ghostly nun, but that the pub building had once been a nunnery.

At the Cunningham's invitation, The Congleton Paranormal Society held an vigil at the pub the night of 14th/15th January 2006. During the course of the night, the group's medium managed to contact four spirits and learned something of their lives. They were the spirits of a twelve-year old girl named Susannah; of a man called Henry who was very angry because he had been struck on the head; of a 58-year-old woman, Sarah Elizabeth Thorley; and a 58-year-old travelling odd job man Ben, who lived in the first half of the 19th century. There was, however, no contact with the spectral nun Sarah, and, therefore, no opportunity to discover whether she is the original Swettenham ghost or a different spirit.

TILSTONE FEARNALL

A dip in the A51 close to the hamlet of Tilstone Fearnall is haunted by the ghost of a monk. Some reports speak of it as being 10 ft in height. There have been a number of sightings over the centuries but, apart from the reasonable inference that during his lifetime the monk served at a nearby now-ruined priory, nothing is known about the spectre's background. No story survives to explain why this particular shade should be condemned to linger at this lonely spot when all his brothers have long since departed for their rewards.

The dates of the ghost's appearances do not seem to have been recorded, but they have been frequent enough for the dip to become known locally as 'The Haunted Hollow.'

TUSHINGHAM

What must be Cheshire's strangest haunting is reputed to have occurred at Tushingham's Bluebell Inn, where the spectre was that of a duck.

Unfortunately, there is no documentary record of the time when these events happened, nor of the names of the folk involved, or even the name of the duck. What is certain is that the story is very old, and may even date back to the 14th-century inn which occupied the site before the present timber-framed building was built in 1667.

According to tradition, at some time in the distant past, the landlord owned a pet duck. This duck annoyed the customers by pecking at their ankles, until the stage was reached where it became obvious that something had to be done. A trial was held, and the bird was found guilty, executed, and buried. Unfortunately, even this extreme measure failed to solve the problem. The duck's ghost rose from its grave under the floorboards and resumed its attacks.

A duck's ghost is said to be imprisoned at the Blue Bell Inn, Tushingham.

Faced with this new emergency, the landlord turned to the church for help. Twelve priests were assembled and, under the battering of their united prayers, the ghostly bird was reduced to a size where it could be pushed into a wine bottle. The bottle was then corked tight, and sealed into a wall.

WINSFORD

The Gym at Winsford is haunted by what is probably the only amorous ghost in Cheshire. Soon after they started work on converting the former Wesleyan chapel into a fitness centre in 2002, Jason and Michelle Young began, separately, to realise that there was something strange about the place.

'Nothing big at first – just little things like pens going missing or objects being moved,' Michelle recalls. 'With all the chaos I thought it was just me being absent-minded.'

For his part, Jason was puzzled by a series of power stoppages. The building had been completely re-wired, but there were inexplicable failures in the lighting and heating. Even more disturbing, he was assailed by a feeling that someone was following close behind him, when there was no-one to be seen. And, somehow, he sensed that it was the ghost of a woman. A firm sceptic on all matters paranormal, he struggled to clear his mind of the ridiculous idea – without success. Instead, the impression of a woman dogging his footsteps became ever more vivid. He realised finally just how vivid that impression had become on an occasion when he went into the lavatory and caught himself turning on his invisible follower with the words, 'I'm having a pee, go away!' 'I didn't tell Michelle at the time because I didn't want to scare her,' he explains.

Then there was the ghostly cuddle. For some three months, while they were searching for a house close to the Gym, the couple were obliged to commute from their home at Barton, 10 miles away. When

The Gym, Winsford.

they worked late, they often slept overnight in the staff room on the first floor. Sometimes they both worked late; sometimes it was just Jason. On one occasion, when Jason slept alone at the Gym, he was awoken in the middle of the night by the sensation of being pressed gently, but firmly, down into the mattress. The former commando found he was hardly able to move a muscle. Again, he was obliged to protest to a ghost he was reluctant to believe existed. 'Let go of me,' he demanded from between gritted teeth. 'It's not funny!' Immediately, the pressure was released.

On another occasion, when Jason and Michelle were both sleeping at the Gym, they were roused at 6 o'clock in the morning by a loud knocking on what they thought was the front door. 'I thought we'd overslept and a member of staff was waiting to get in,' says Michelle. As they both dashed downstairs, Jason realised, from the sound, that the knocking was not on the outside front door, but on the second or inside front door. When they reached it, they were staggered to find that there was no-one to be seen, and that both front doors were still locked.

It was then that Jason told Michelle about his ghostly experiences. His revelations caused her to realise that her own problems could well have been caused by something other than absent-mindedness. Discussing the matter, they began to wonder whether there was more than one spirit in the building.

And so it went on, with many, apparently supernatural, interferences in different aspects of work at the Gym. It even seemed that some supernatural agency was showing approval or disapproval of some members of staff. There could be little doubt that Jason's invisible follower was very well disposed towards him but, apparently, the part-time yoga instructor was not so fortunate. The yoga classes were held in the former Sunday school room on the first floor. When the room was not in use, the temperature was not noticeably different from that in the other parts of the building, but immediately the yoga classes started, it plummeted. All attempts to raise it by turning up the heating failed. The problem was so serious that it brought the yoga course to a premature end. But, at a later date, when the room was used for pilates classes the temperature remained normal. Could it be that a ghost or ghosts had taken a dislike to the yoga instructor?

Matters finally came to a head one night in early 2005. As Jason was about to leave the building after completing his closing-up routine, which included unplugging the treadmills, he heard the unmistakable sound of a treadmill machine switching on. When he returned to the area where the machine was located he was confronted by an unnerving sight. 'As I watched, the treadmill started running. Then it went faster and faster, and the heart-monitor came on. I double-checked and the power was off. It freaked me out and I just bolted.' Later, he wondered whether some spirit or other was expressing its displeasure at the location of that particular machine.

It was that incident which prompted Jason and Michelle to ask rescue mediums sisters-in-law Christine Hamlett and Jackie Dennison for help. 'The presences didn't seem malevolent,' recalls Michelle, 'but I wanted to know who our uninvited members were.' Jackie and Christine arrived at the Gym, by appointment, and Jason introduced them to Michelle's mother, Brenda, who is also a medium. With the help of their spirit guides, Jackie and Christine contacted the spirit of a woman, who said her name was Miriam and that she had been a Sunday school teacher at the chapel. She said that she had lost her lover in the First World War, and that she had been following Jason about the gym because Jason reminded her of him.

Brenda then confirmed Jason and Michelle's theory that more than one ghost haunted the building by saying that she could see a stern-looking man standing behind Christine. She discovered that his surname was Walker.

The mediums also encountered the spirit of a young boy named Thomas. About six years old and fair-haired, he was wearing grey trousers and a dark jacket. He said he was very scared of the stern-looking man. Jackie and Christine helped him to escape by crossing over to the other side.

When Jackie followed up the work at the Gym, by looking through the chapel records at the library, she discovered that a Miriam Heath had been a Sunday school teacher at the chapel in 1907, and that a Robert Walker had been the chapel minister during the early years of the 20th century.

'Michelle and I were both gobsmacked when Jackie came up with the proof,' says Jason.

Jackie Dennison believes that, like Thomas, Robert Walker has now crossed over to the other side, but Miriam remains in residence. She does not follow Jason around quite so much, but she still makes her presence felt from time to time. There was, for example, the occasion when Michelle's brother, Daniel Bush, a full-time instructor was searching for a particular document in a filing cabinet. He knew he had placed it there, but he just could not find it. Michelle thought she knew the reason. She spoke sternly, 'Miriam, if you're hiding that paper, it's not funny. Put it back!' When Daniel opened the cabinet again, a moment or two later, he found the paper in a place where he had already looked.

The haunting has not harmed Jason and Michelle's business. Far from it. Many members are fascinated by the situation.

WRENBURY

Wrenbury lies some five miles to the south of Nantwich. It is an ancient village clustered round a delightful triangular, green. And it is haunted. That is, there are enough witness accounts to suggest that it has a large, ghostly population, spread across all parts of the village. Shades have been seen or made their presence known in the church, in the churchyard, in a pub, in the post-office, in the (former manorial) hall, in various houses, at a footbridge, and on some of the roads and lanes.

In his very readable and persuasive book, *The Ghosts of Wrenbury*, local historian John Pound outlines the results of numerous interviews

The village of Wrenbury as seen by local historian and artist John Pound.

with fellow residents who have been involved in paranormal encounters, together with his own experiences of the supernatural. The number of incidents he mentions runs well into two figures. Even so, there are many sceptics. Some, indeed, who have been involved in strange incidents which defy all other explanations, but still cling to their disbelief. Like the Wrenbury woman who was making her way to bed one night when she passed someone she thought was her husband walking in the opposite direction – she presumed he had forgotten something. When she reached the bedroom, however, he was already in bed. They searched the house from top to bottom, but found no one. Both doors were locked and bolted, and all the windows were fastened. Years later, the witness still had no doubt that the incident had occurred, but she still refused to believe that it could possibly have been of supernatural origin. Curiously, nothing else of a similar nature occurred in the remainder of the twelve years the couple occupied the house.

Such isolated single-witness incidents pose problems for the researcher. Had the witness hallucinated? Had they fabricated the experience? Even so, there are occasions when the witness is of such a clear-minded and prosaic nature and of such unimpeachable honesty that their reports must be treated seriously.

Witnesses like Nora Riding for example, a former hospital matron and a woman not given to flights of fancy. For some 15 years during the 1980s and 1990s Nora and her husband, Derek, lived in Elm House, a late-16th-century oak-framed building overlooking the village green.

One night Nora awoke to see the figure of a man, well-dressed in the Jacobean-style, enter the bedroom through an ancient doorway which the Ridings had recently re-opened to reach a bathroom. She watched calmly as the figure moved to the foot of the bed, and stopped to inspect her and the sleeping Derek. Then it beckoned in the direction of the bathroom. A second figure, that of a boy, emerged from the bathroom, and joined the man figure at the foot of the bed. The lad stared open-mouthed at the Ridings for a moment, before the ghostly man waved him away angrily. The man made what Nora described as an apologetic gesture, before following the boy out through the other door. The whole episode took place in complete silence.

Nora had not been alarmed. She observed the episode from beginning to end with clear-minded interest, and the following morning she was able to recount it, in detail, to Derek. The man figure, she recalled, had worn a flowing hat, while the ghostly boy was in rags. She was emphatic that she been wide awake the whole time, and that it had not been a dream.

Another problem which challenges the paranormal researcher in many investigations is that of establishing the spirit's former human identity. There can be no doubt that the most satisfactory sort of outcome to any ghost inquiry includes the recording of the spirit's former name together with some details of its life. In some cases the information has already been established, but in many others – perhaps the majority – it is unknown and likely to remain so. For example, the possibility of identifying the two ghosts observed by Nora Riding appears to be remote.

Elm House, Wrenbury.

Just occasionally, however, an investigator's efforts are rewarded by the sort of success which attended John Pound's research into the ghost of Wrenbury Green. It was a success achieved by collecting fragments of information over some 15 years, and then piecing them together to establish the identity of the ghost and to clarify the background story.

Again, the haunting involved the Ridings' home, Elm House. John learned from an elderly resident that, from time to time, the shade of a young woman dressed in white has been seen flitting from the old house to a farmhouse on the opposite side of the green. Immediately, he was reminded of a story told to him some time previously by Derek Riding. A former engineer and, like his wife, a prosaic sort of person, Derek had been perplexed by a strange experience which had occurred to him on several occasions.

When the Ridings moved into their house, one of its rooms housed a village corner shop. One morning, Derek was crouched down under the glass counter re-arranging his display when he heard a woman's voice call out, 'Good morning Mr Riding.' He answered her but, when he stood up, he found the shop was empty. Puzzled, he looked about the ground floor of the house, but there was no-one there. He then searched upstairs, only to find that he appeared to have the house to himself.

Some weeks later, again when he was crouched down behind the counter, the same thing happened. 'Good morning Mr Riding,' called the same voice. Again, the shop was empty.

On both occasions, it was if the words were deliberately spoken when he was alone and could not observe their source. It was as if a trick was being played on him. The ghost – for such it seemed to be – repeated the joke on a few more occasions over the following months but then stopped, as if she had grown tired of it. Derek described the voice as quite ordinary, and without any distinctive accent.

The story led John Pound to wonder whether the playful ghost and the shade which flitted across the green to the farmhouse could be one and the same. He collected the next clue at a school fête, some years later. He had occasion to speak to two elderly ladies who told him that it was members of their family, Thomas and Ann Jennings, who had opened the shop at Elm House. They also told him that the couple had suffered a tragedy when their daughter, who had been courting the son of the farmer at the farm on the opposite side of the green, died suddenly. They did not, however, know the girl's Christian name or the cause of her death.

Still, it was progress. Persuaded by the mention of the courtship that it could be the ghost of Jennings' daughter who crosses the green to look for her lover, John searched the local churchyard for her grave. Without success. The only Jennings' grave was that of a family which had lived in Sheppenhall Lane; not on the green. The parents' names, too, were different. Very obviously it was not the right grave. He had reached an impasse.

Until, that is, the spring of 2005 when he was introduced to Mrs Margaret Kenyon. In the course of their conversation it emerged that her mother had been a Jennings. Learning of his interest in the Wrenbury Green Jennings, she consulted her family records, and was able to tell him that they had all been buried at Whitegate, near Northwich. The parents' Christian names were Thomas and Rose Anne, and the daughter was also named Rose Anne. The end of John's long quest came with the information that 21-year-old Rose Anne Jennings had died of meningitis on 15th February 1920.

So, thanks to John Pound, the identity and background of the Wrenbury Green ghost has been established. Her story is a sad one but, if she is the same spirit who teased Derek Riding, she is obviously not completely bowed down with grief.

The shop was closed some years ago, and the Ridings have left Wrenbury. The present occupiers of the house have experienced nothing in the way of paranormal activity.

•Index•